Kissing Animals

Animal Smackers

Kissing Animals

Animal Smackers

Text by
Claudia Tödtmann

Benedikt Taschen

This book was printed on 100% chlorine-free bleached paper in accordance with the TCF standard.

Hohenzollernring 53, D-50672 Köln

Adaptation: Michael Hulse
Design: Eberhard Wolf
Cover design: Angelika Muthesius
Composition: Utesch Satztechnik GmbH, Hamburg
Printed by Neue Stalling GmbH & Co KG, Oldenburg

Printed in Germany
ISBN 3-8228-9321-8
GB

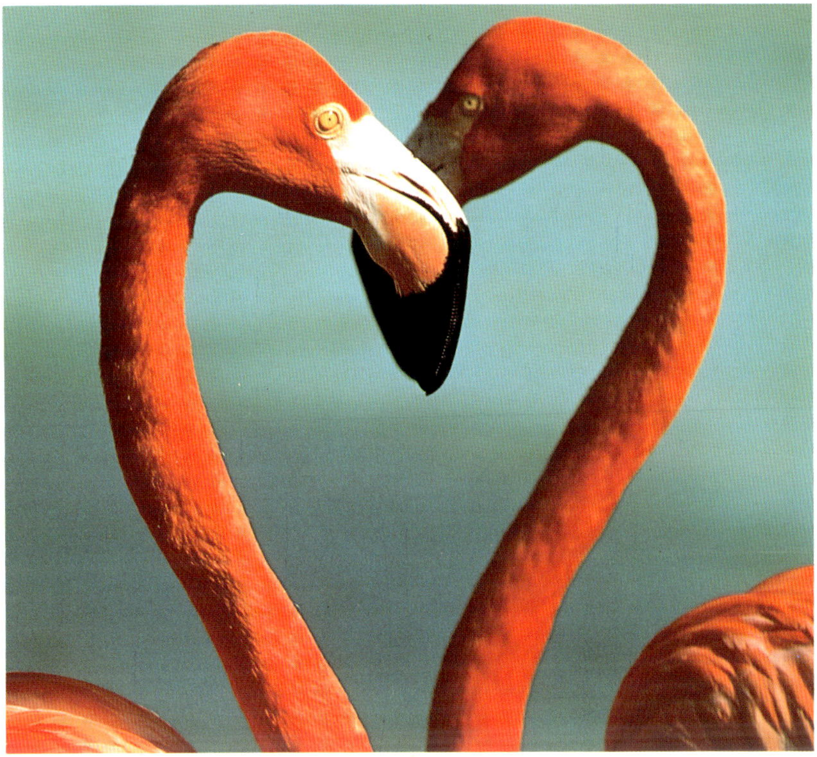

Kiss kiss

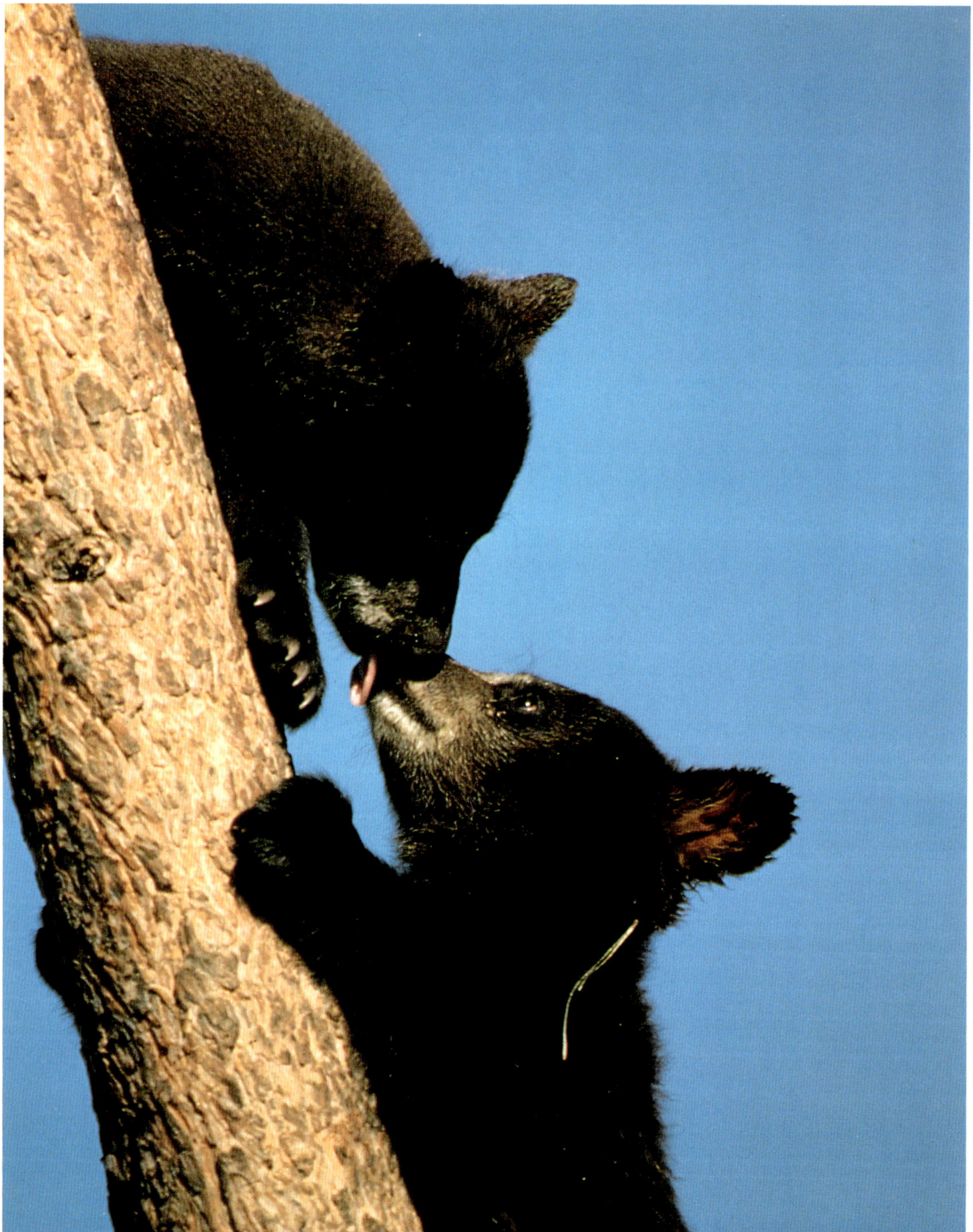

Pecking, licking, billing and cooing

You have to kiss a lot of frogs before you find your prince – if you ever do. The fairy tale princess who transformed an ugly frog into a handsome young prince, married him, and lived happily ever after, must have been a fairly unusual person to be kissing frogs in the first place. Generally speaking, if frogs are kissed it tends to be by other frogs. This book is about what happens when two frogs, or flamingos, or hoary marmots, get together – what you might call animal smackers.

The fact is that kissing is by no means an exclusive privilege of the human race. Animals too show affection by kissing. A budgerigar may snuggle against Grandma's cheek, or a horse may nibble its rider's hand affectionately. Scientific research has proved that kisses have the same function for animals as for humans. Anthropologist Jane Goodall, studying the behaviour of chimpanzees in Gombe National Park (Tanzania), found that they too kiss for various reasons according to the situation – to show submission, or as a greeting, or, of course, to herald a bout of romantic monkeying around.

The word "kissing" may not always be appropriate, of course. A lot depends on the build of the animal. Birds peck, elephants entwine their trunks, frogs and fish gawp, and doves bill and coo. Throughout the entire animal kingdom, kissing is an expression of tenderness and, of course, sexual desire. During foreplay, elephants thrust their trunks into each other's mouths. Brown hyenas and eared seals greet each other by pressing their muzzles into the corner of the other's mouth. Chimpanzees greet with a kiss, and the lascivious bonobo (a species of chimpanzee) can actually French kiss.

Do you come here often?

So too, if poets can be believed, do bees. "The moth's kiss, first!" wrote Robert Browning. "The bee's kiss, now!" Some snakes go in for French hissing, expressing endearment with their tongues. Giraffes show affection by rubbing necks, and a horse will lovingly nibble its companion on the back. In the case of fish, research has not come up with any conclusive answers yet, though it is beyond dispute that no fish has ever been caught with lipstick on its collar. As for polyps – perhaps they nuzzle onto each other's suckers?

Love at first sight is no human speciality either. Research done by animal physiologists on tupaya tree shrews in South East Asia shows that when they are smitten it is much like love at first sight. Their kiss is a greeting lick, during which they sniff and make their mark on each other – their equivalent of exchanging rings. From the moment they kiss, they spend a lot of time together, and produce offspring. Interestingly, the effect of all this harmony is to lower the heart rate, and the animals live longer than they would have done with no one to kiss.

Research on humans to date has merely shown that single people do not live as long as married people. Kisses do have a beneficial effect on road safety, though. Traffic research has shown that a kiss before setting off to work has an extremely positive effect on the driver, putting him in the right frame of mind and thus affecting the quality of his driving. Whether it absolutely has to be a loving partner's kiss, or whether a slobbery lick from the dog will do the trick as well, we don't yet know.

Kisses are not only said to increase life expectancy. They are in themselves deeply symbolic of

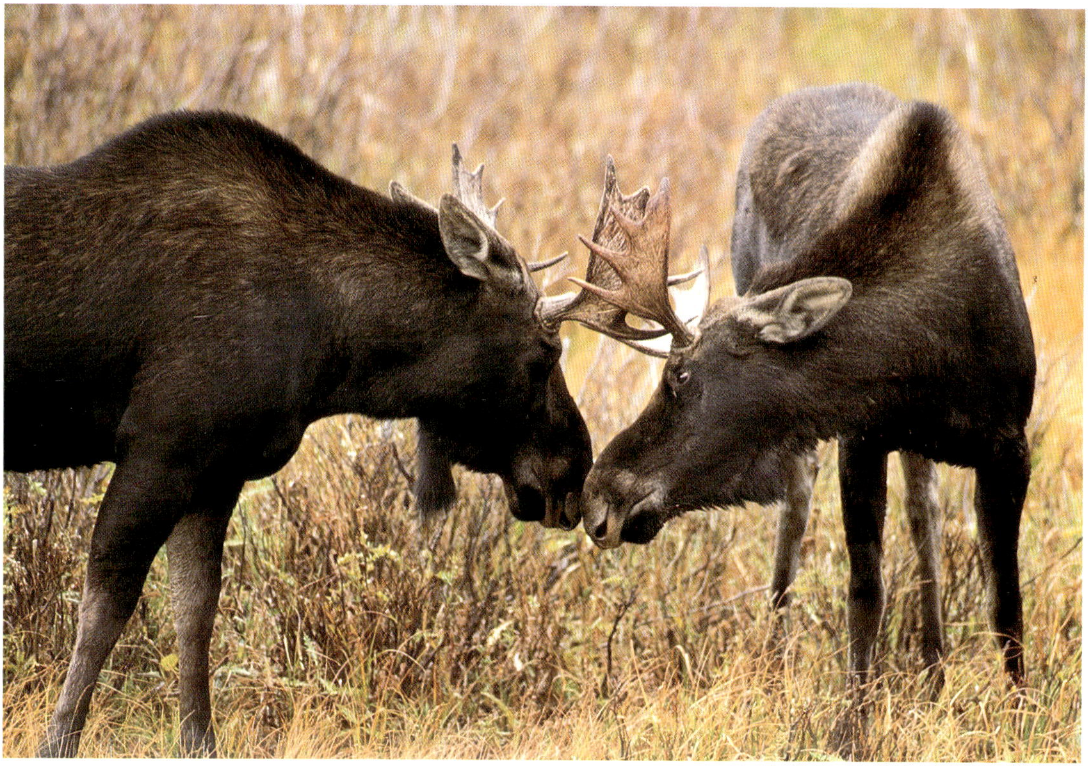

life: not for nothing do we speak of the kiss of life, not for nothing does the prince revive Sleeping Beauty from her deathlike hundred-year sleep with a kiss. A kiss revitalizes us. It is electrifying. It fires us with the joy of living. "Sweet Helen," cried Christopher Marlowe's Faustus, "make me immortal with a kiss!" More prosaically, drowning people and avalanche victims are revived by mouth-to-mouth resuscitation.

Kissing supposedly originates in the mouth-to-mouth feeding common among animals. The mothers feed their young pre-chewed food by regurgitating it directly into their mouths. This can best be seen in bird families, where the parents slave away all day cumbersomely fetching home one worm after another to their brood. The bigger the little ones get, the more strenuous the feeding becomes for the parents, since the youngsters require bigger and bigger portions. This may sound pretty familiar from commuter belt experience, where the bigger portions come with designer names and higher price tags, but at least human mothers are spared the regurgitation.

A baby's suckling at the breast is really a very intensive kiss – and fathers have been known to be quite jealous. Even so, babies do not get used to being kissed so easily. They do not see why they should be slobbered over, and prefer to turn away except on occasions when an emergency demands a consoling cuddle. Once they have grasped the ritual and learned to participate, the only terrors left in store are old aunts caked in lipstick and granddads with scratchy whiskers.

In the world of adult kissing, a passionate kiss can burn up twelve calories and work twelve of the facial muscles, while a French kiss involves thirty-nine mouth, jaw and face muscles. This makes it almost a sport – and helps keep beauty fresh. Every second of the day, 866,055 people the whole world over are kissing. Some seem to think it's a test of endurance. The hardest-working kisser in the *Guinness Book of Records* is Alfred A. E. Wolfram of New York, who kissed 8,001 women in eight hours at the Minnesota Renaissance Festival in 1990 – or one every 3.6 seconds. There ought to be a Catullus Prize for such feats. The Latin poet was insatiable too, and wrote: "Give me a thousand kisses, then a hundred, then another thousand, then a second hundred, then yet another thousand, then a hundred."

A licence to kiss

Author Maryam Sachs may not be a contender for the Catullus Prize, but she must have broken some kind of record when she published a hefty, expensive tome on the history of kissing. When it was launched at a reception attended by four hundred invited guests, almost everyone inevitably felt the appropriate form of congratulation was a kiss. Some, as they say, are more kissed against than kissing.

Similar free-for-alls are common practice at weddings in many parts of the world. If there are any guests who have never yet kissed the bride, they naturally feel their hour has come, a unique opportunity to do so quite openly, with impunity. Of course, the all-important kiss at a wedding is the symbolic kiss that follows the pronouncement "I do" and the exchange of rings. Suddenly the couple have a licence to kiss. Even the priest seems to think so, and pointedly says, "You may now kiss the bride". It's a moment well milked in the movies, and

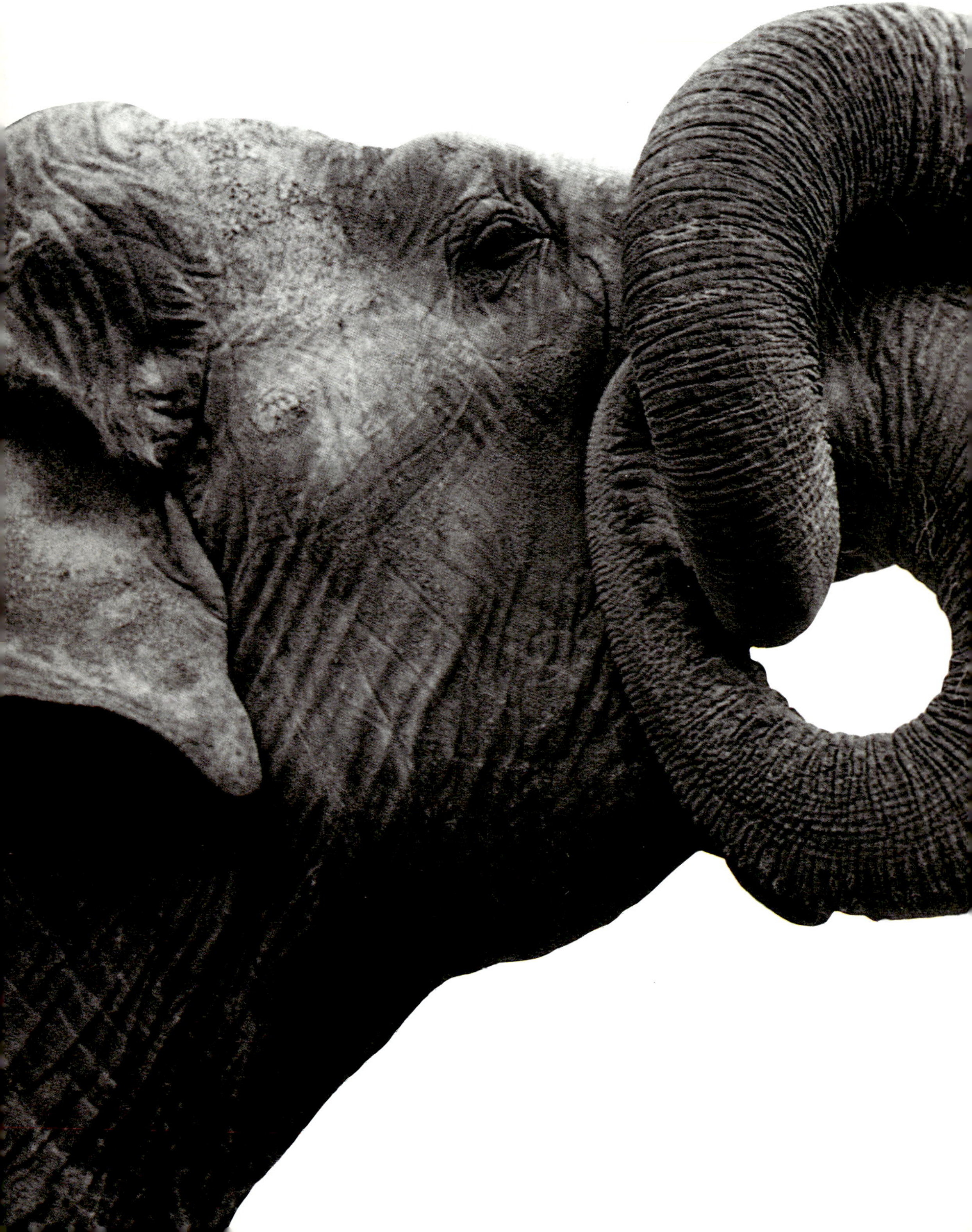

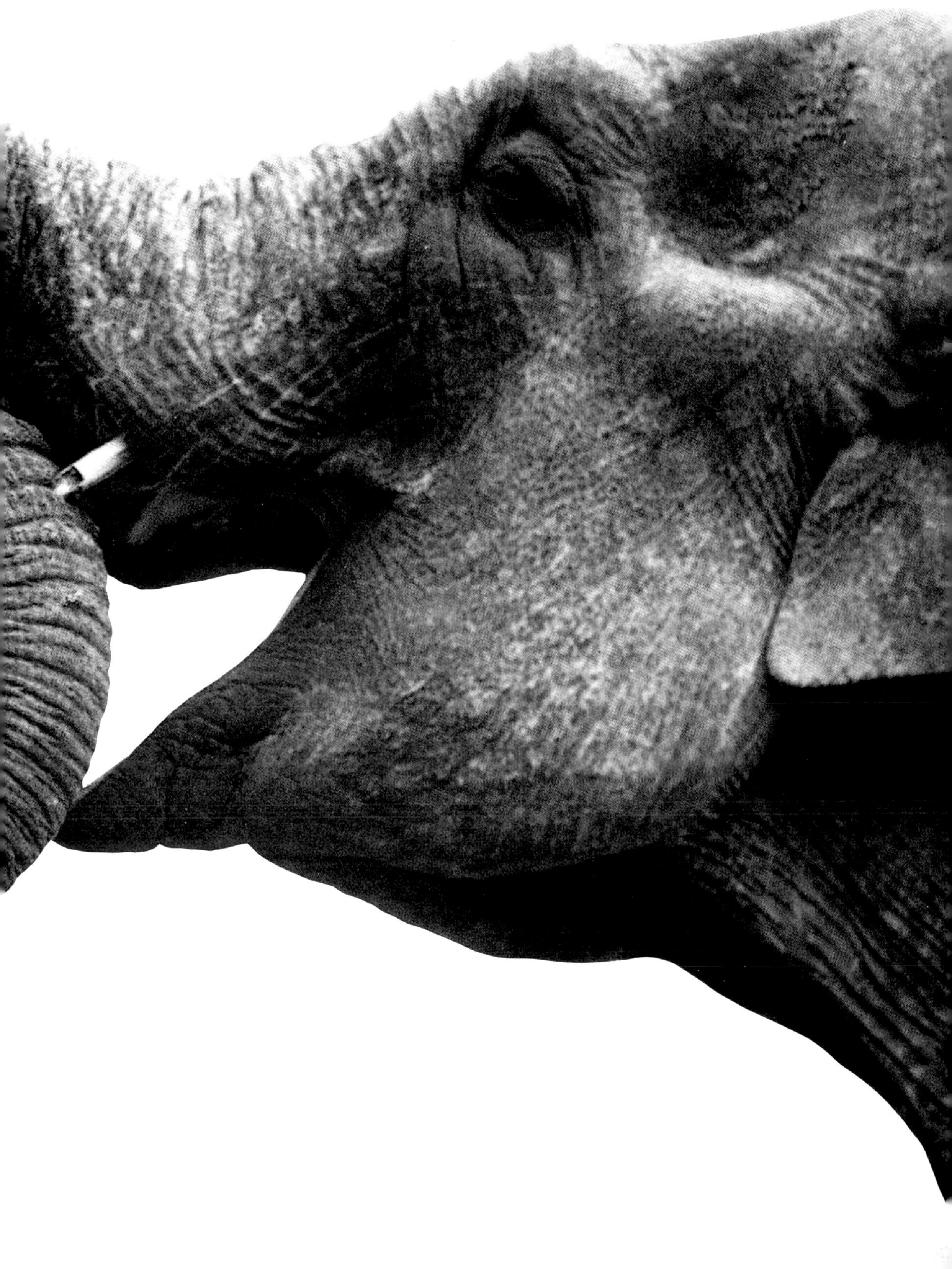

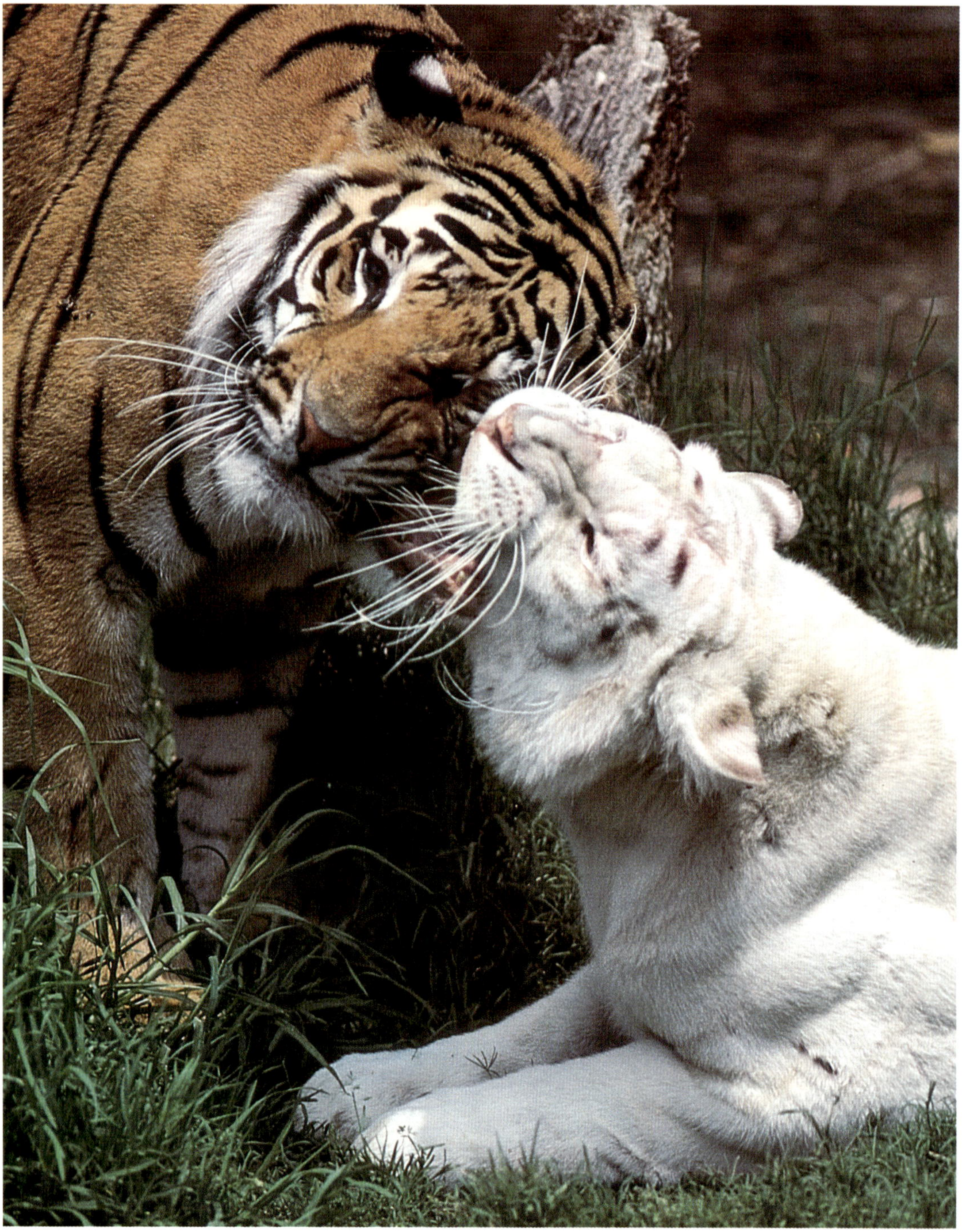

The back row at the movies

as often as not the leading lady will promptly lean back à la Scarlett O'Hara, as if determined to play out her passion to the full, in church.

That kiss is symbolic of the church's sanction of sexual relations between the couple, and references to kissing are often polite ways of avoiding another four-letter word. "It is not a fashion for the maids in France to kiss before they are married", Shakespeare tells us in *Henry V*, but Henry kisses his Kate nonetheless, and swears: "You have witchcraft in your lips." Sir Herbert Beerbohm Tree's famously sharp tongue dismissed an actress more acclaimed as a lover than on the stage: "She has kissed her way into society." Laurence Sterne, the grand master of innuendo, teased his readers richly when he wrote of a maid: "In Paris, as none kiss each other but the men, I did what amounted to the same thing – I bid God bless her." And one wonders whether Alexandra, the fated wife of Czar Nicholas II of Russia, was familiar with this convention when she observed: "They accuse Rasputin of kissing women etc. Read the Apostles; they kissed everybody as a form of greeting." (She was right about the Apostles, of course. In Romans, 16, 16, we read: "Salute one another with an holy kiss.")

Talking of saluting, it was in "You're in the Army Now" that the longest kiss in film history was fought out, in 1941, between Jane Wyman and Reg Toomey. It lasted a full, fruity three minutes and five seconds. What on earth did the cinema audience do to pass the time? What the couple on screen were doing was perfectly plain, but for the audience it must have seemed an eternity. For viewers in the TV age the marathon snog provides an opportunity, like commercials, to make a cup of tea, go to the bathroom, or zap across to see what's on the other channels.

Cinema audiences, of course, don't necessarily simply sit back and watch. Audience participation is the idea, and in the cosy dark cinema many a couple will be having as much fun as the stars on the screen. At one time cinemas in many places even featured love seats, minus the troublesome arm rests that usually separate couples. The Hungarian-born humourist George Mikes once wrote: "One of the most popular American entertainments is kissing. Young men and young girls pull up on the highways and kiss each other between 6.30 and 10.30 p.m. This kind of amusement is considered perfectly decent, probably because it keeps you from going to a cinema." Mikes presumably had a fairly steamy idea of what went on in the back row at the movies.

In films, the most significant kisses always spell the beginning of the end. First the kiss, then the credits. Countless movies clinch the wrangles or manœuvres of the lovers with a kiss, and take it as a tactful pretext to exit from the story. The most famous screen kiss was probably Rhett Butler and Scarlett O'Hara in "Gone with the Wind", but Marilyn Monroe and Tony Curtis weren't bad in "Some Like it Hot" either – even if Curtis later admitted, "She was so cool I felt like I was kissing Hitler."

It was another film, "Pretty Woman", that made common knowledge of a fact normally known only in certain circles: that prostitutes usually prefer not to be kissed by their clients. "Pretty Woman" made Julia Roberts a star overnight – though a body double in fact stood in for some of the more passionate moments. Prostitutes do not kiss their clients

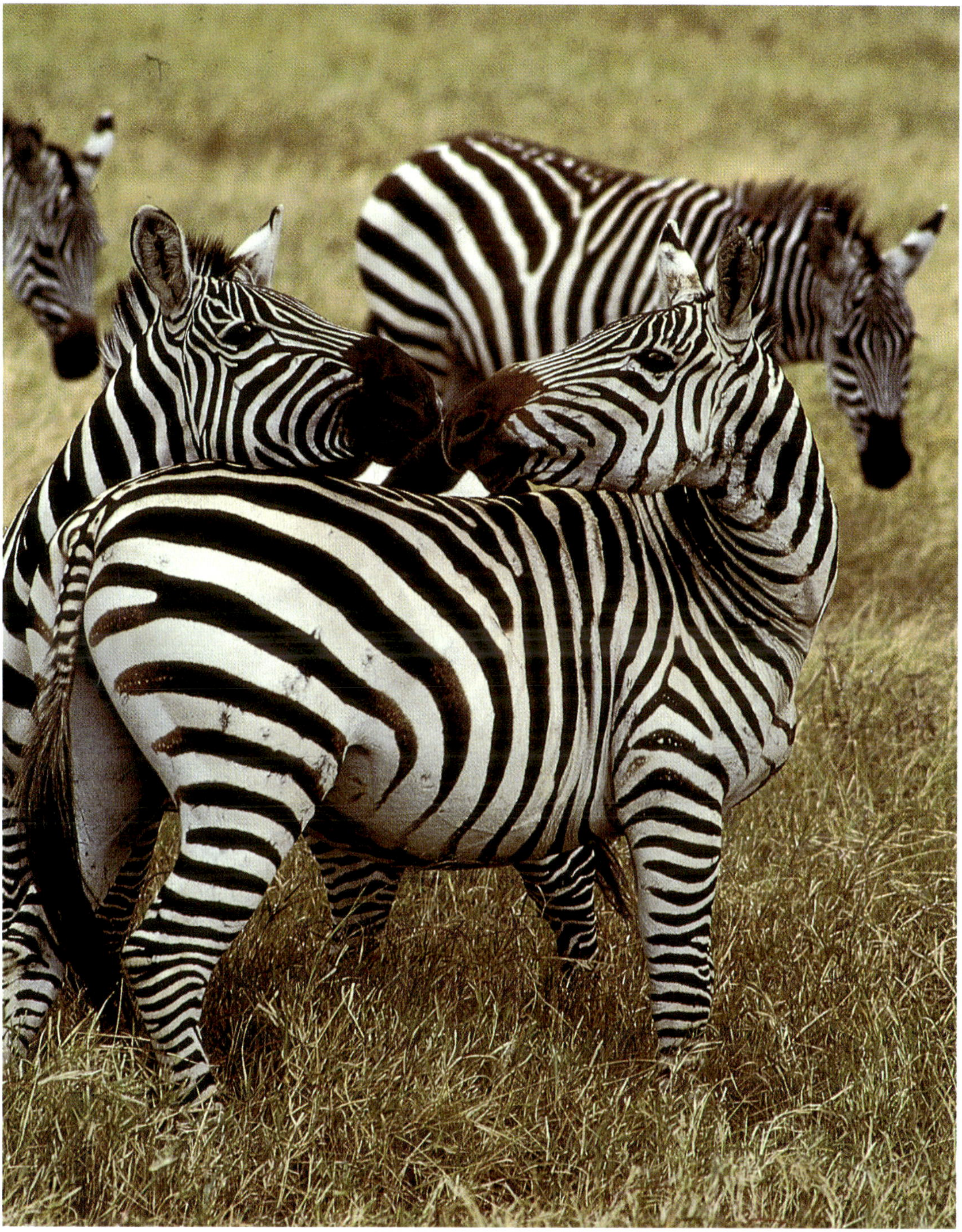

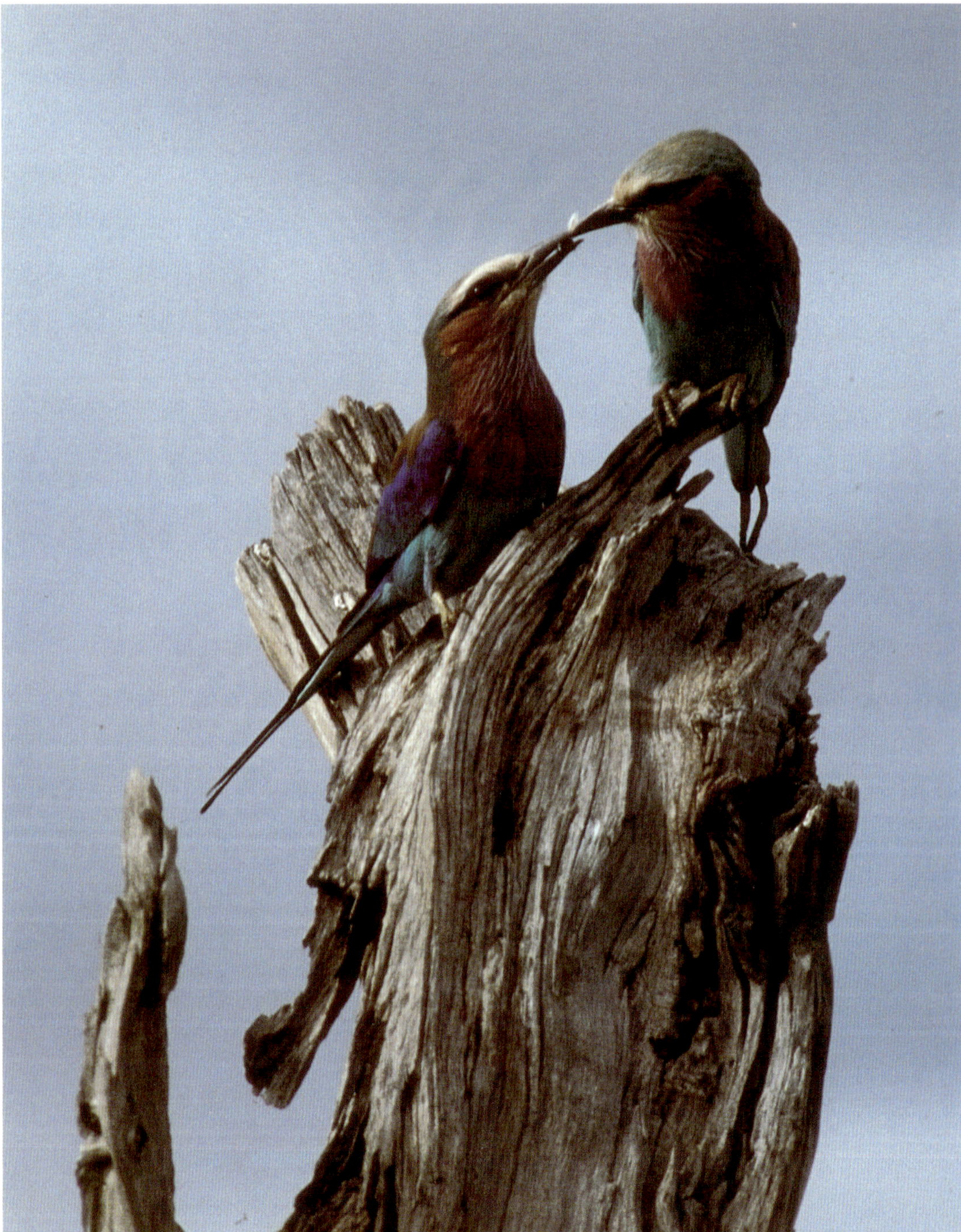

because it is too intimate, and reserve kissing for their true partners. Rudyard Kipling knew this when he made one of his soldiers say: "I'm sick of the hired women. I'll kiss my girl on her lips." The fact is that a kiss is widely felt to be the gateway to the soul, and even to symbolize the breathing-in of life into a body (despite the fact that the God of Genesis does this through Adam's nostrils). A kiss carries such a symbolic charge that it can come to mean more than the act of love.

Left, right, and left again

Kisses can also be gestures of submission – say, when a vamp orders a client to kiss her boots (and the client excitedly obeys). A kiss can express reverence: Pope John Paul II, the joke goes, known for his habit of kissing the ground (or rather the runway) whenever he alights from a plane, can tell the airports of the world by their taste. And kisses can also signify the desire for peace – especially among politicians. Two who were not especially known for their promotion of world peace, Erich Honecker and Leonid Brezhnev, conspicuously gave each other brotherly kisses on the mouth whenever they met. And US President Harry Truman quickly discovered: "The President spends most of his time kissing people on the cheek in order to get them to do what they ought to do without getting kissed."

Brotherhood is the name of the game: a kiss oils the wheels of society, and puts the seal on friendship. The trendies and yuppies of the world are great kissers, and all over Europe embarrassments pile up daily as people used to planting two kisses on Parisian cheeks realise they're expected to deliver three (left, right, then left again) among the Walloon Belgians and Dutch. To non-kissing societies such as Britain, where even too firm a pat on

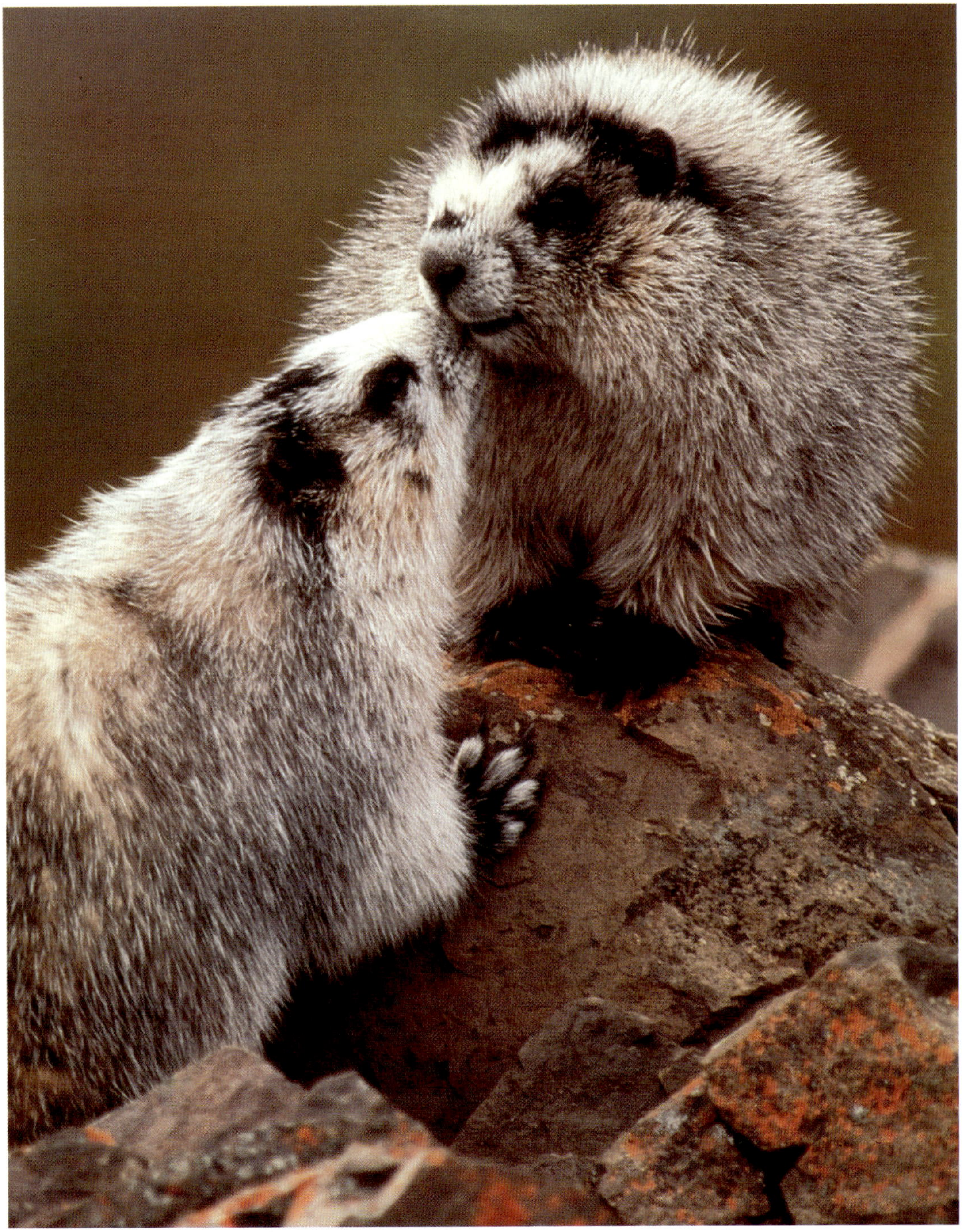

the back may embarrass the male of the species, continental determination to smooch can seem over the top, especially when it becomes clear that the less you know someone, the more you kiss them. But it all goes back to that ancient Christian rule – "Salute one another with an holy kiss" – which has survived longer in the more Catholic parts of Europe. Similarly, in places where the old church festival of the Shrovetide carnival has survived – from Rio to the Rhineland, from Venice to Trinidad – the convention of kissing looses its bonds and becomes an elaborate game of sexual shadowplay, with the rules suspended, kisses showered like confetti, and (in Germany) the ladies cutting off the men's famous phallic symbols, their ties.

Social kissing is a complex art. A smacker on the cheek betrays the amateur; a real professional's kiss is a hint, a waft, a mere breath of air. "If a kiss on the cheek is correctly wafted," declares German journalist Heinz Joseph, "only the cheeks of the parties involved will touch, and the discreet smack will drift past the lady's ear into the air. Only an absolute beginner might accidentally swallow his lady's ear-ring." The same applies to kissing a hand, gloved or no: etiquette demands that a wafer of air remain between the gentleman's lips and the object of his desire. The gentleman, incidentally, may always kiss the hand of a married lady, but if she is unmarried he ought not to (so the etiquette manuals pronounce) unless she is over thirty-five. And the ladies should only kiss the hands of other ladies, as a sign of respect, if they are at least two generations older. It would be helpful, presumably, if persons anxious about these matters would always carry their birth certificates about them.

"You have witchcraft in your lips."

(William Shakespeare)

Lip service

But it is not only lovers and friends and Mediterranean types who kiss. Ever since Judas, the kiss of betrayal and enmity has been the very definition of deceit. The misuse of the kiss is seen as appalling in every culture. And, by the same token, the power of its positive associations is so great that kissing is used by the advertising industry the whole world over, to sell everything from alcohol to chocolate. Lipsticked female lips'll shift it. Cosmetics companies invariably claim their lipsticks are kiss-proof, and invariably they aren't. Yet men still seem to be particularly attracted by bright red lips, and over half of all French women apparently go nowhere without their lipstick. So the old jokes about men's shirt collars will be with us for a while yet.

The Inuit (Eskimos) presumably find lipstick pointless, since they don't kiss on the lips anyway. The Inuit kiss by rubbing noses – and so do many peoples in Polynesia, Tonga, Malaysia, Borneo, Samoa and New Zealand. For the Inuit, at least, the practice has utterly practical reasons: Inuit women use their mouths for jobs like cleaning oil lamps, softening animal hides, and cleaning their husbands' socks. Their mouths, in other words, are used for everyday tasks, and not in great demand for the emotional business of kissing.

Kissing in public, by lovers, tends to be a touchy subject. In Europe (unlike Japan or China) it is more or less acceptable, though old-fashioned books on etiquette still reject it. The experts on manners also seem to agree that a younger person should wait to be kissed, and that a man should not embrace his wife first. Whether anyone does it by the book any more is a moot point. One rule, though, does seem very welcome: that gum chewers

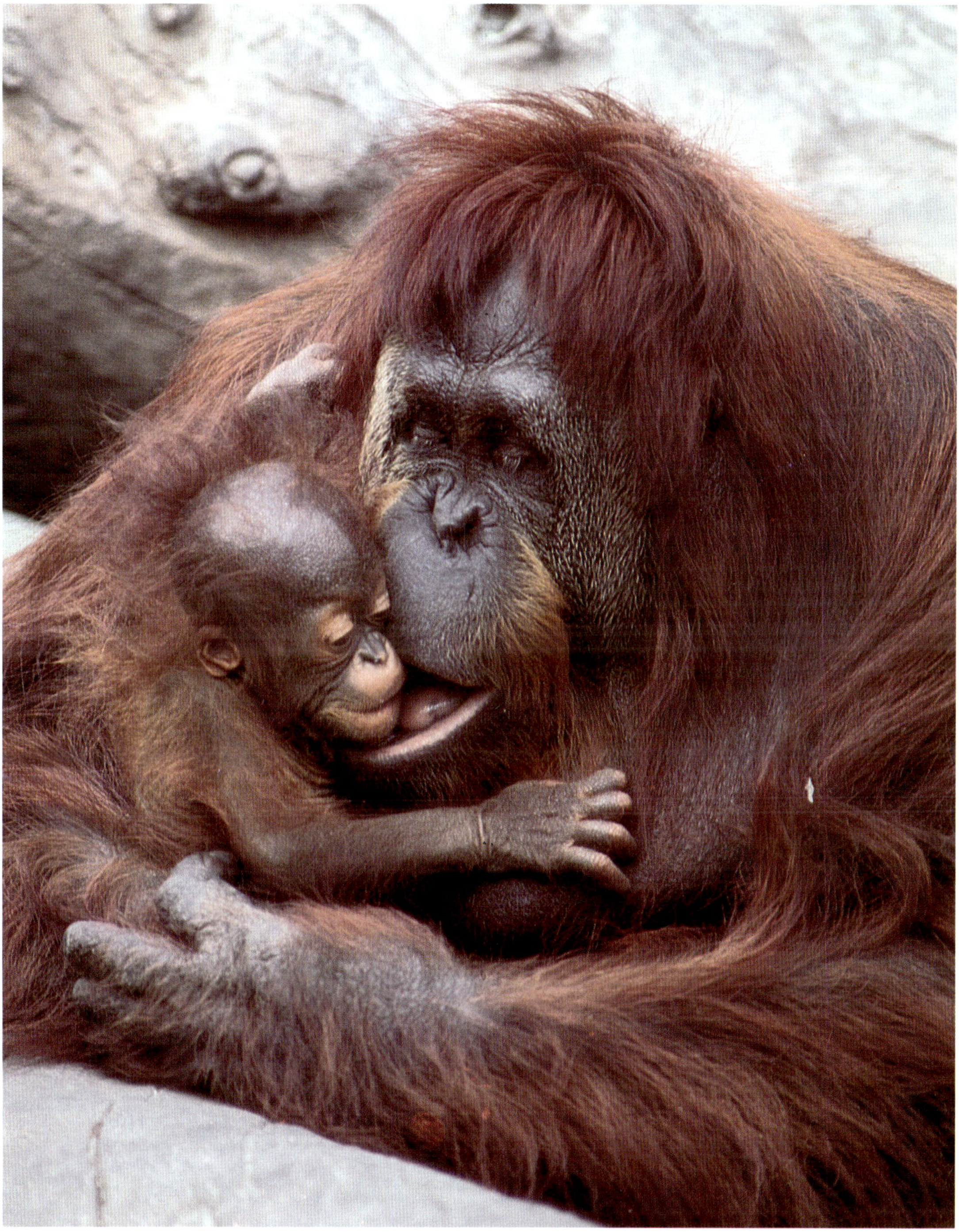

should take their gum out of their mouths before offering social kisses (not to mention the more intimate kind).

No one ever forgets the first kiss – not Mummy's or the whiskery granddad's, that is, but the first time they touched the lips of a member of the opposite sex. It may not always be utterly exhilarating, needless to say. Most people feel nervous, and the whole thing can be quite a test of courage. Illusions may be shattered. Glasses may get in the way, or noses. The wetness of the affair may recall a drooling boxer dog. And the sudden intrusion of a tongue can be startling even for the more practised lover – in his autobiography, Errol Flynn graphically recalled his bewilderment when Bette Davis, screen-kissing him as the cameras rolled, plunged her tongue halfway down his throat.

In "Gentlemen Prefer Blondes", Anita Loos' witless and calculating heroine declares: "Kissing your hand may make you feel very, very good but a diamond and saphire bracelet lasts for ever." For most uncynical people, the very, very good feeling is what counts, and if the kiss isn't given it can always be stolen – which makes it sweeter. True, an entire microbiological world moves from mouth to mouth when we kiss: streptococci, staphylococci, lactobacilli, the lot. (And when Snoopy lavishes kisses on Lucy, who knows if the risk of rabies can be safely ruled out?) Even so, the doctors say kissing is healthier than shaking hands. Which is just as well, since there's no sign of kissing dying out. From Georgie Porgie to Rodin and Brancusi, the kiss has been the thing – and always will be.

Kissing has its sad and even tragic side as well, though. "Since there's no help, come let us kiss and part", wrote poet Michael Drayton. The farewell kiss is so much a part of life that in the late 1980s Munich city council quite seriously debated the possibility of introducing a kissing lane for drivers, since couples kissing goodbye in their cars were forever causing traffic jams outside the Olympic stadium underground station. The populace promptly dubbed the debate "kiss and ride".

The kiss is a moment of oblivion, of deep communion with the other person, and can seem to include the whole world in a moment. Small wonder that most people prefer to close their eyes; only one in five keep their eyes open to kiss. A kiss can sum up the whole of life, all its passions and joys, its tenderness and tragedy. "I kissed thee ere I killed thee," said Othello…

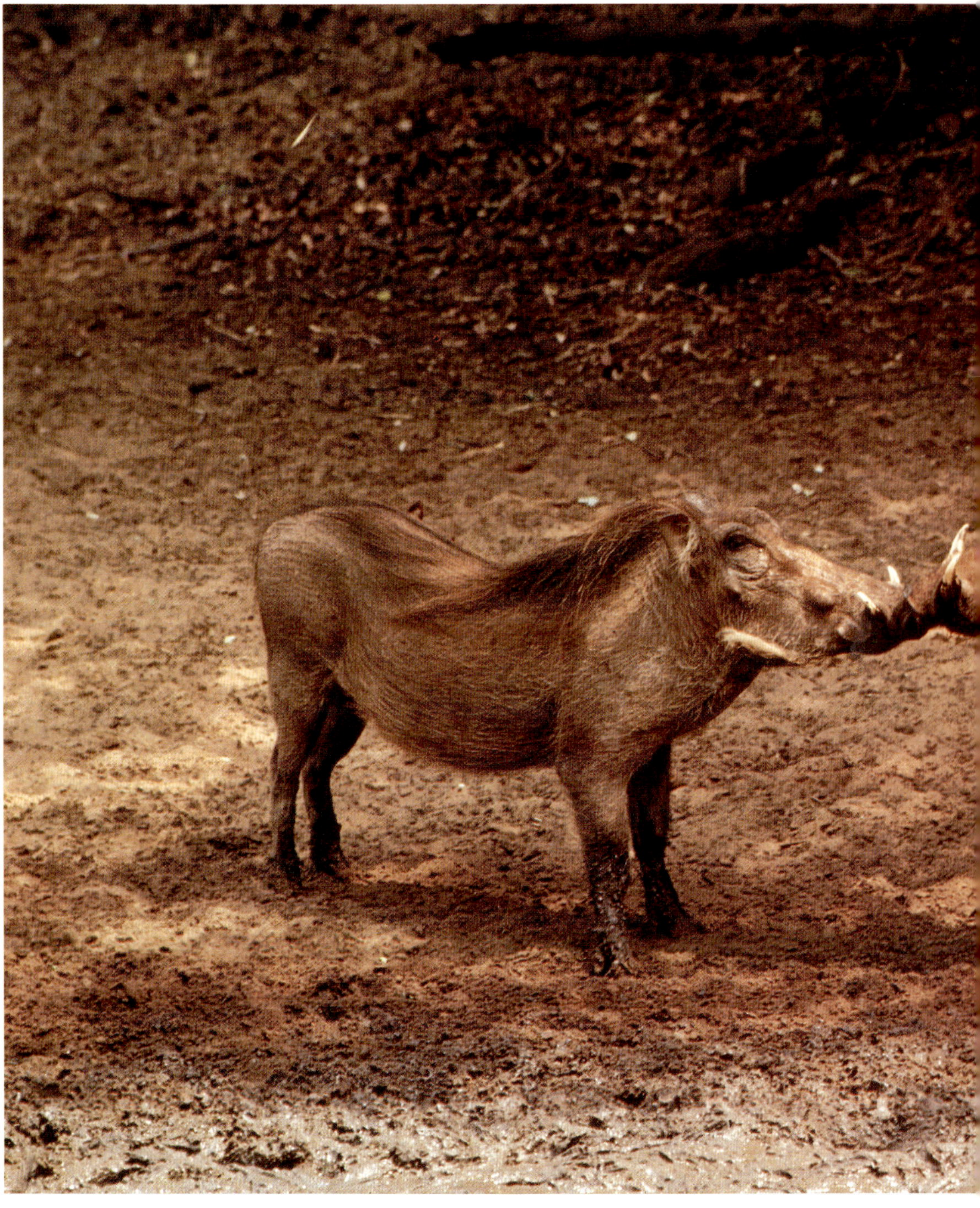

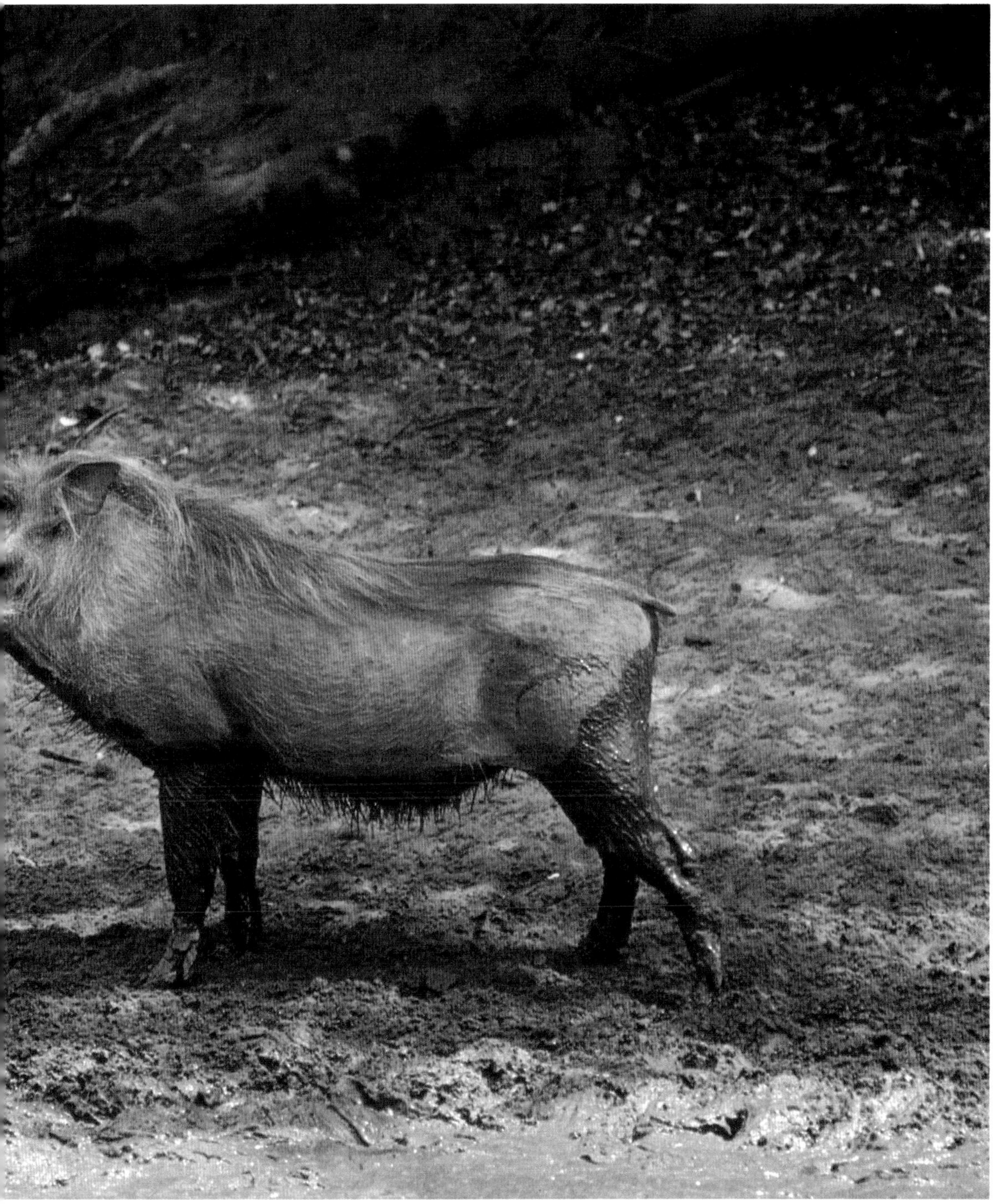

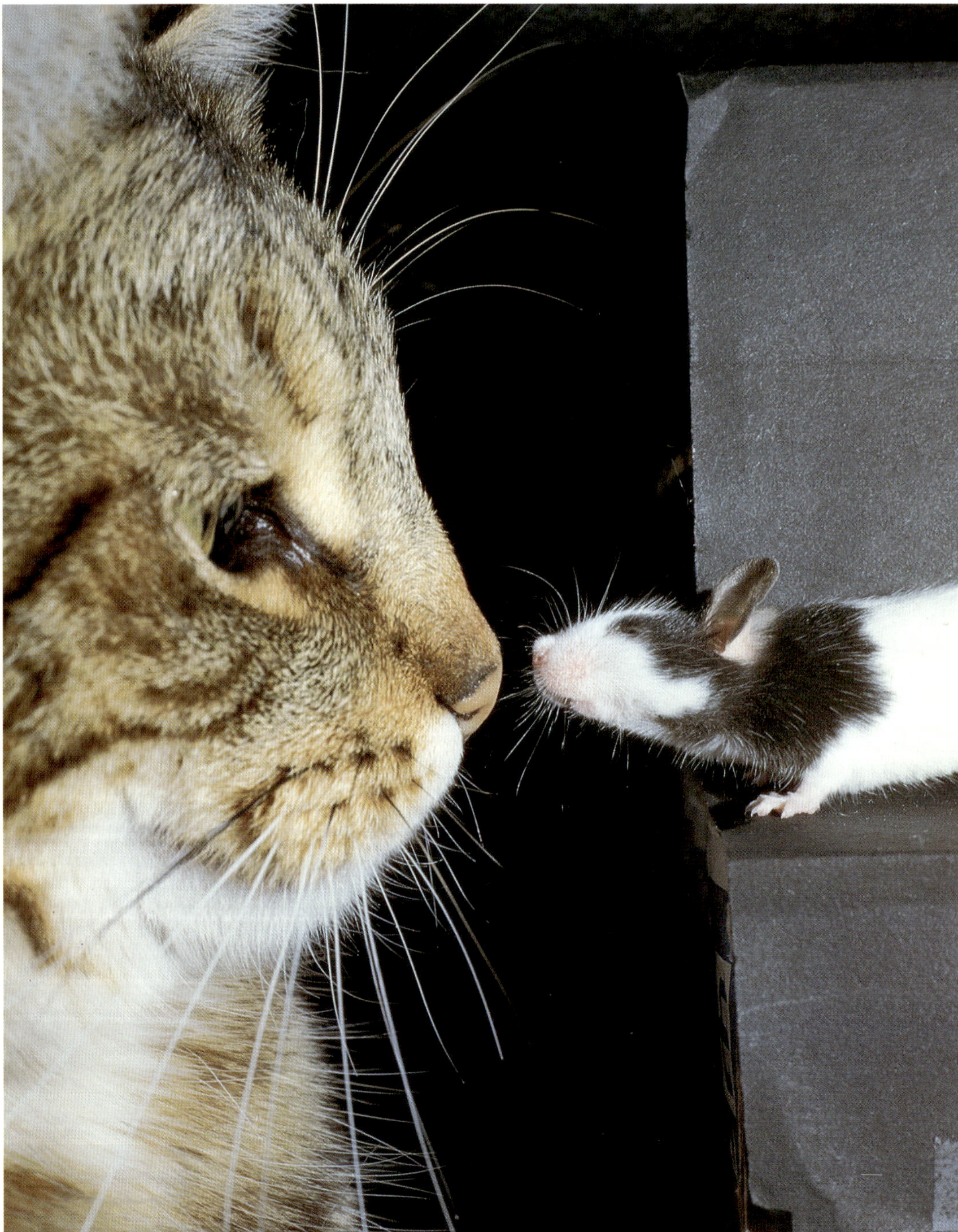

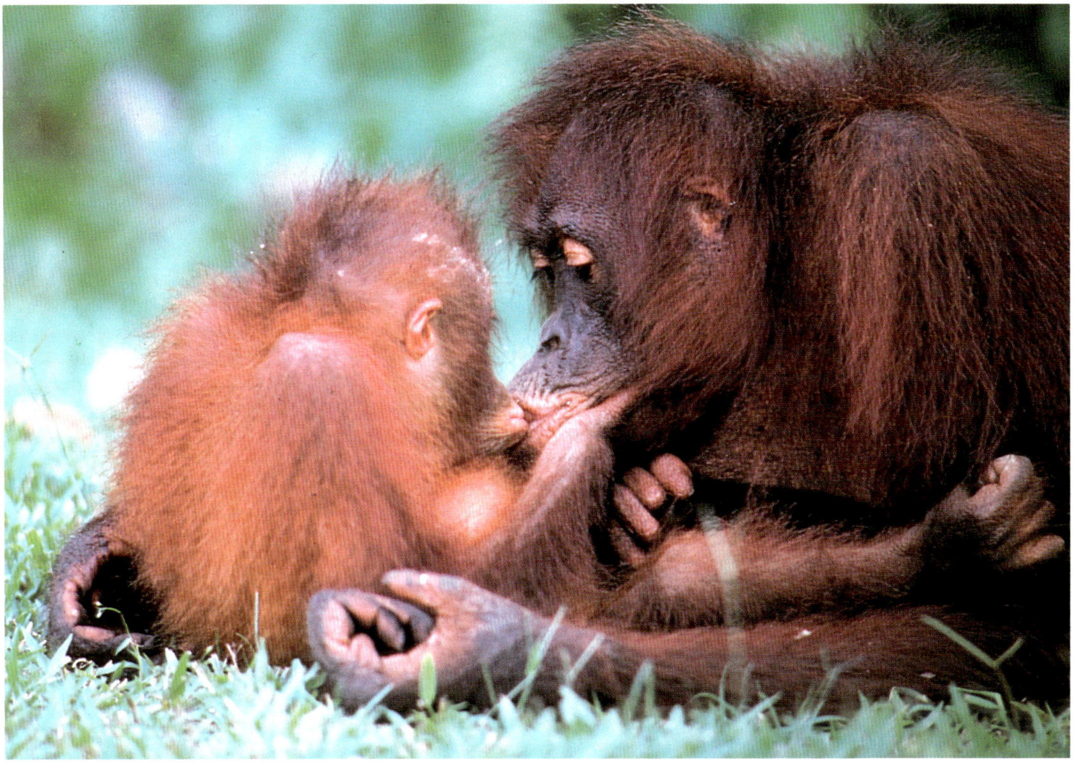

"Kiss thou me, or I'll kiss thee."

(Johann Wolfgang von Goethe)

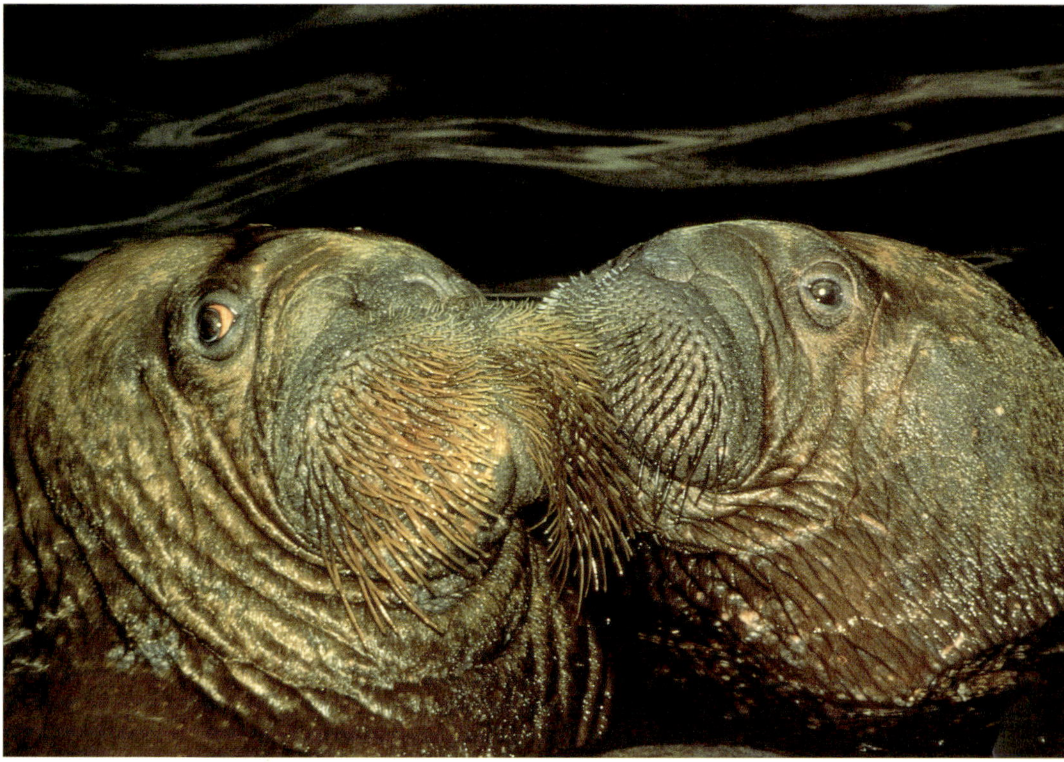

"The worlds arose from out the echo of a kiss."

(Amado Nervo)

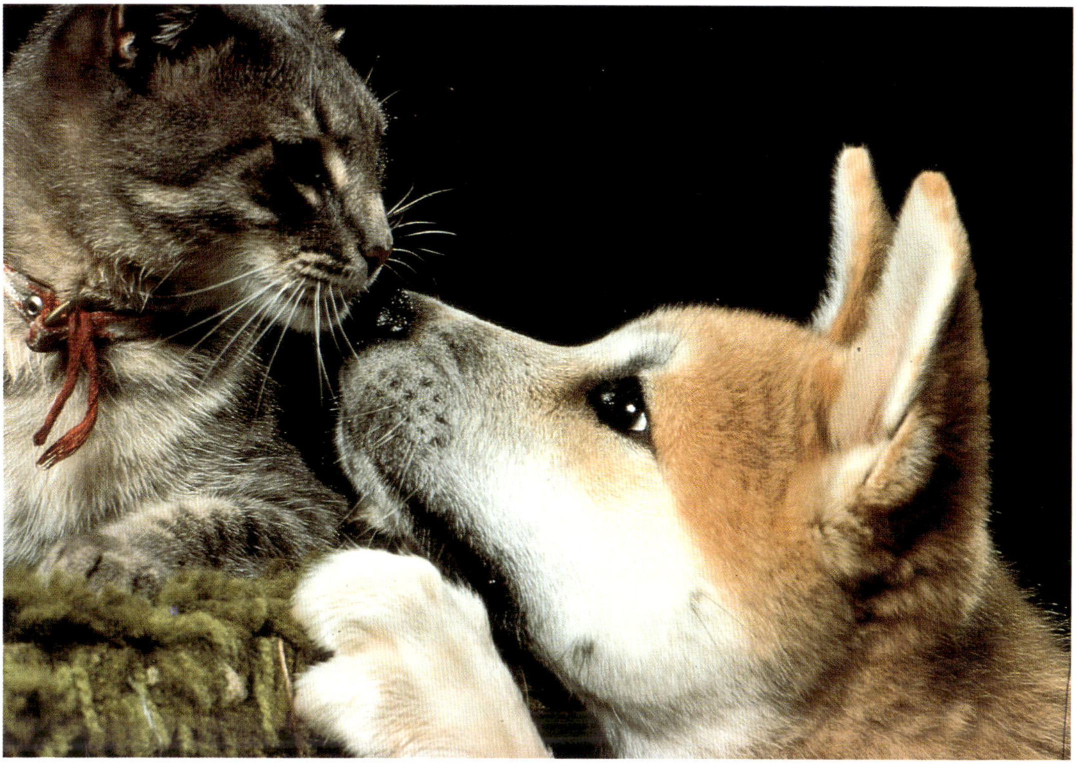

"Kiss me, Kate"

(William Shakespeare)

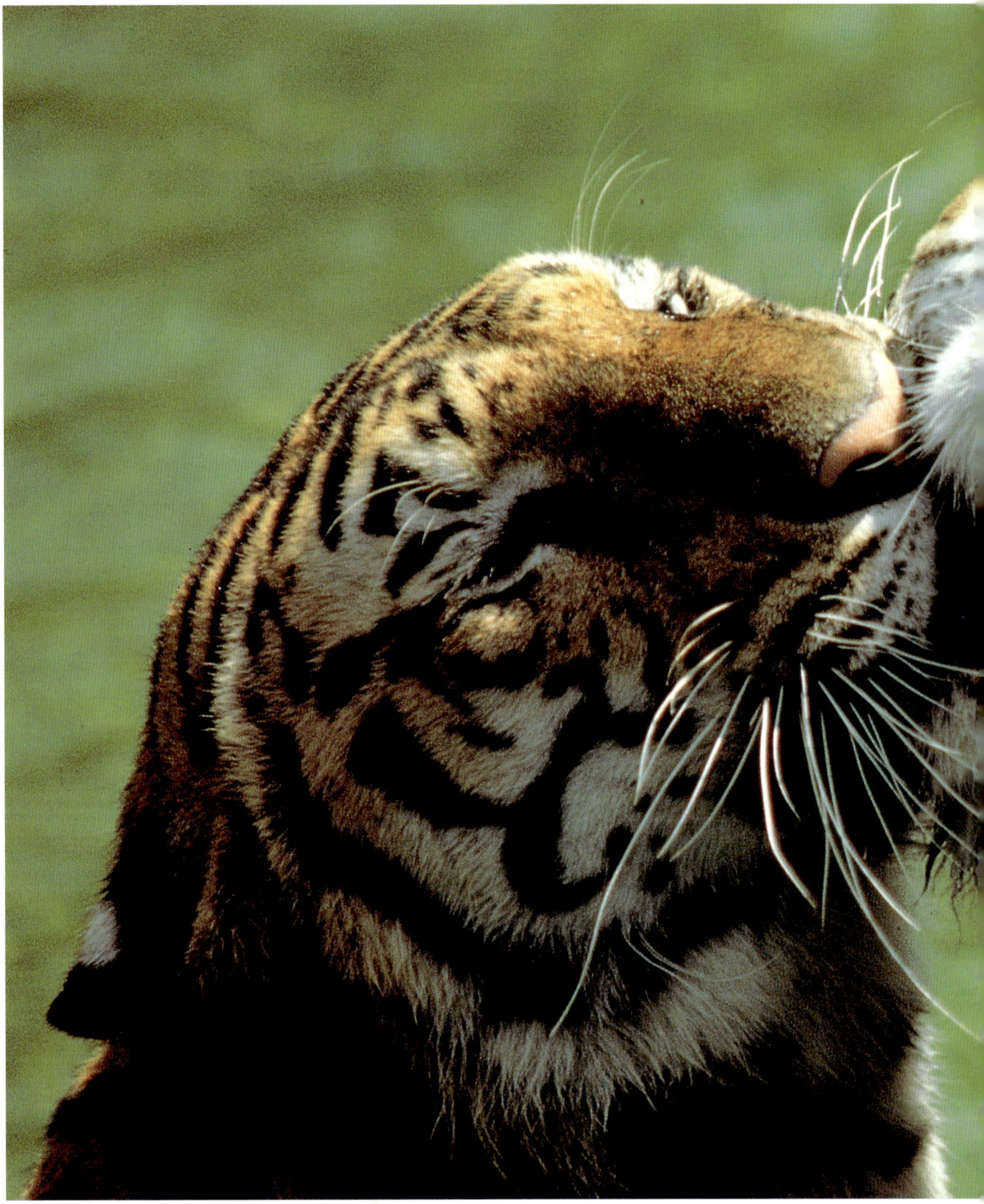

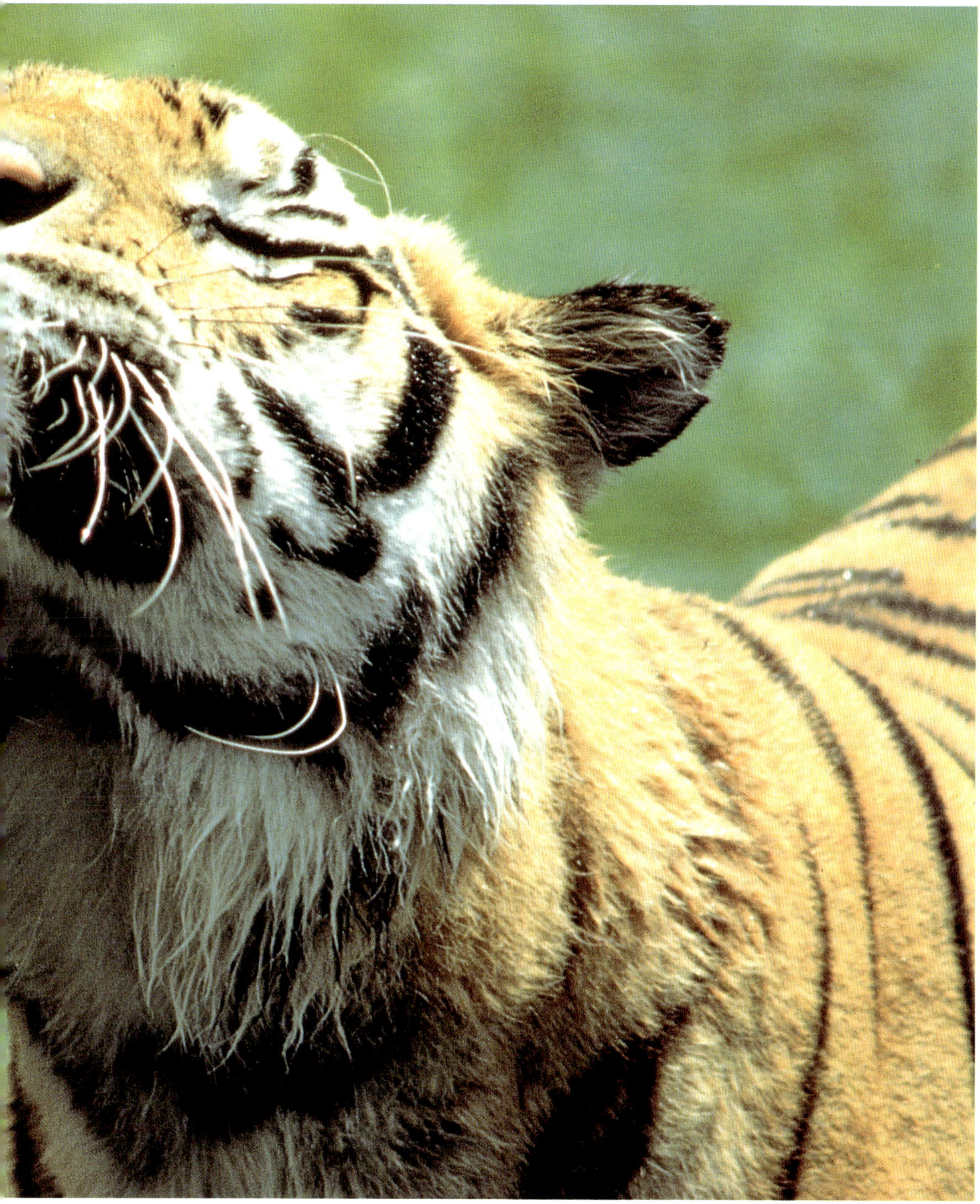

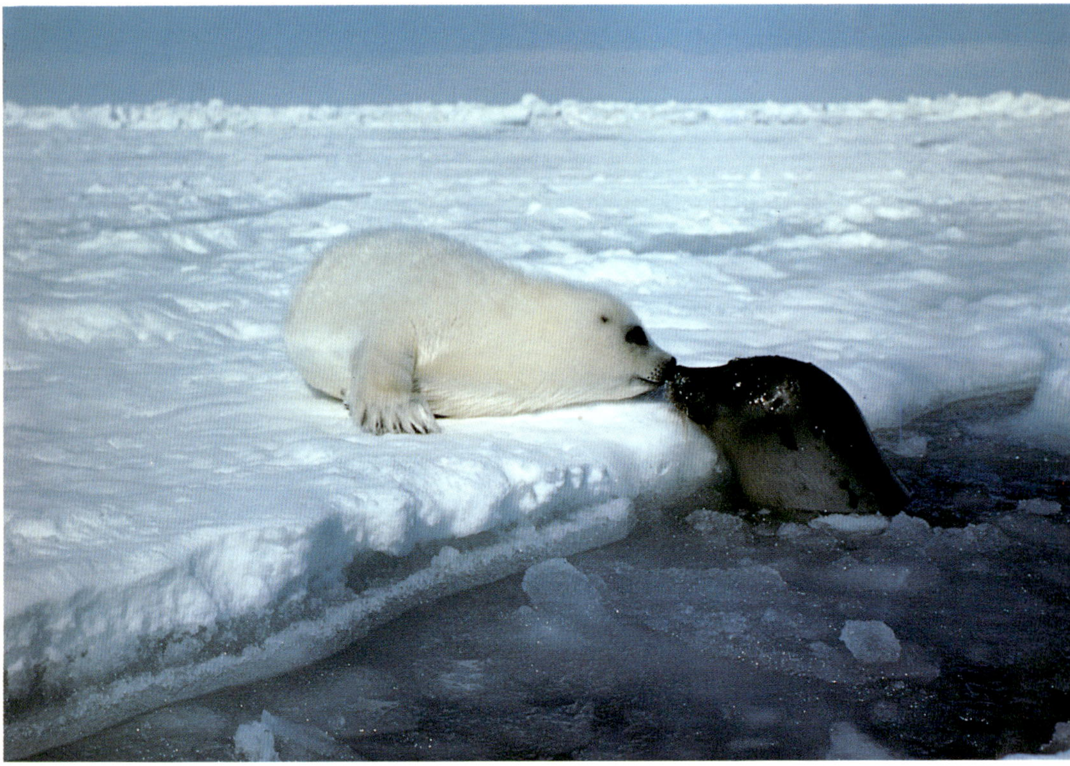

"Ah, how hot it burns, a kiss in the cold!"

(Alexander Pushkin)

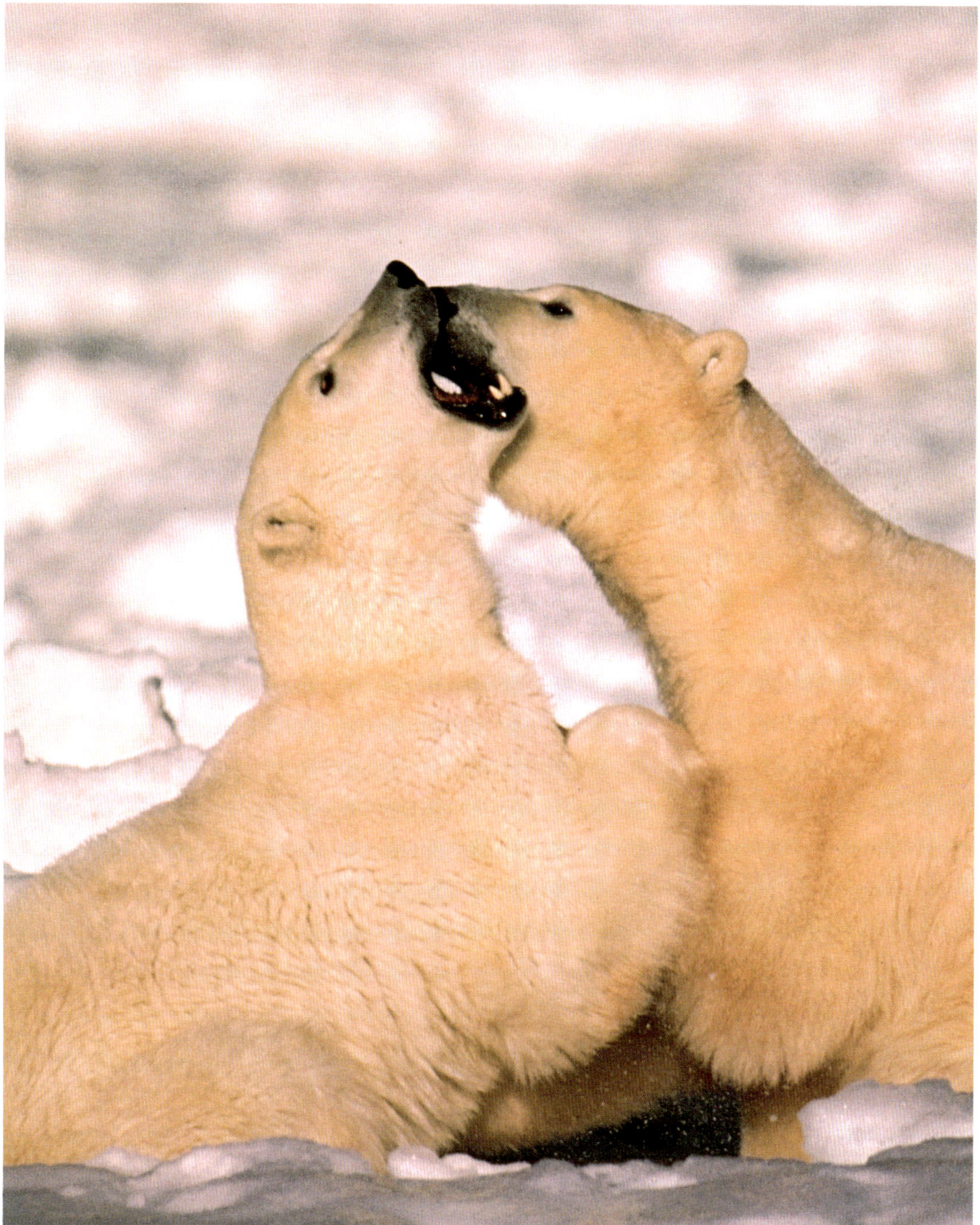

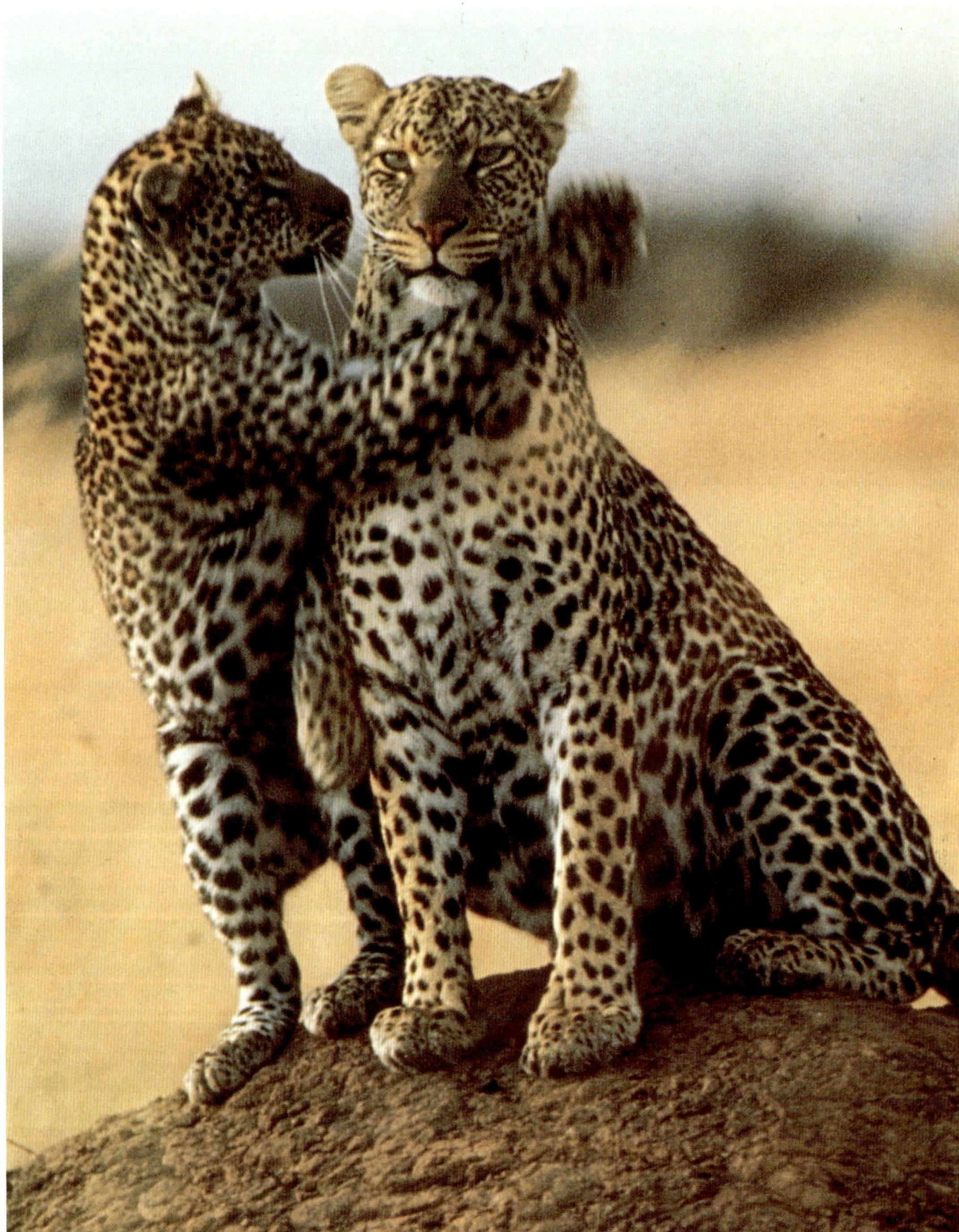

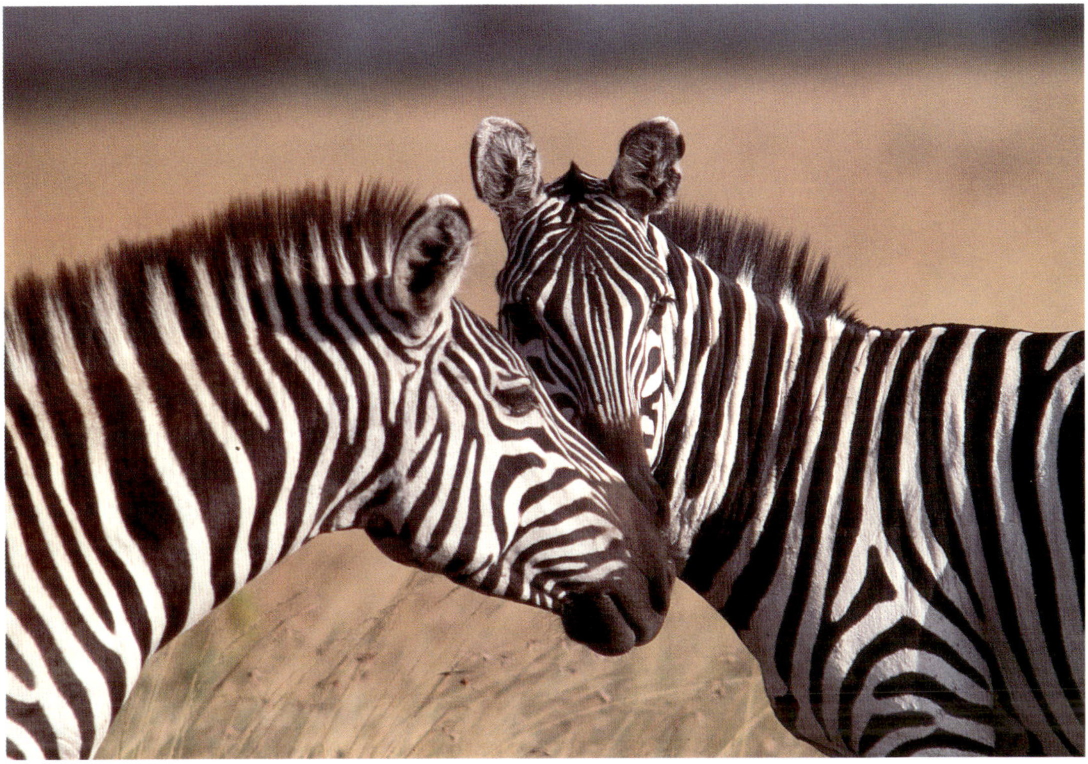

"There are things that can only be said with a kiss, because the deepest and purest of things may never come from the heart but they be summoned by a kiss."

(Maurice Maeterlinck)

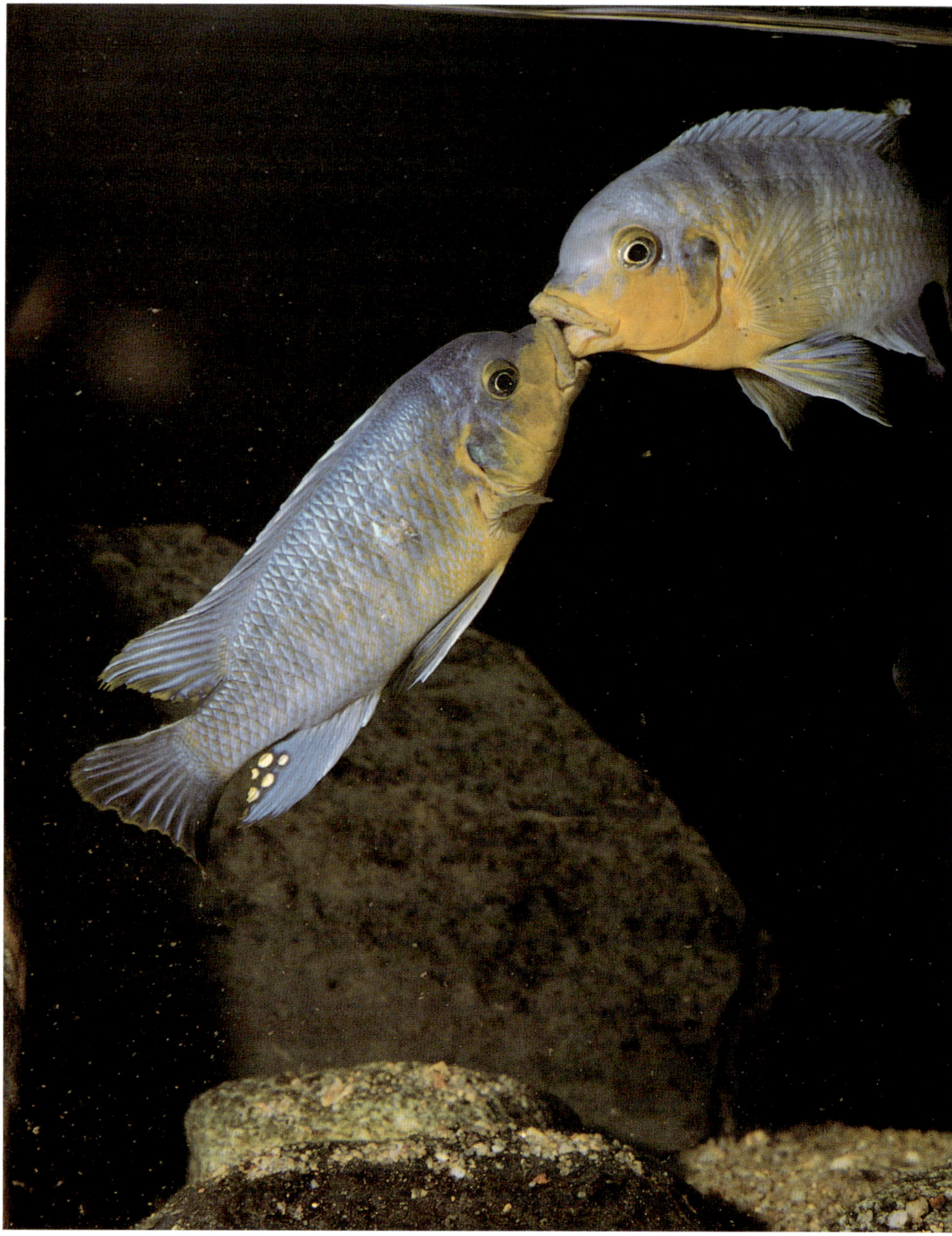

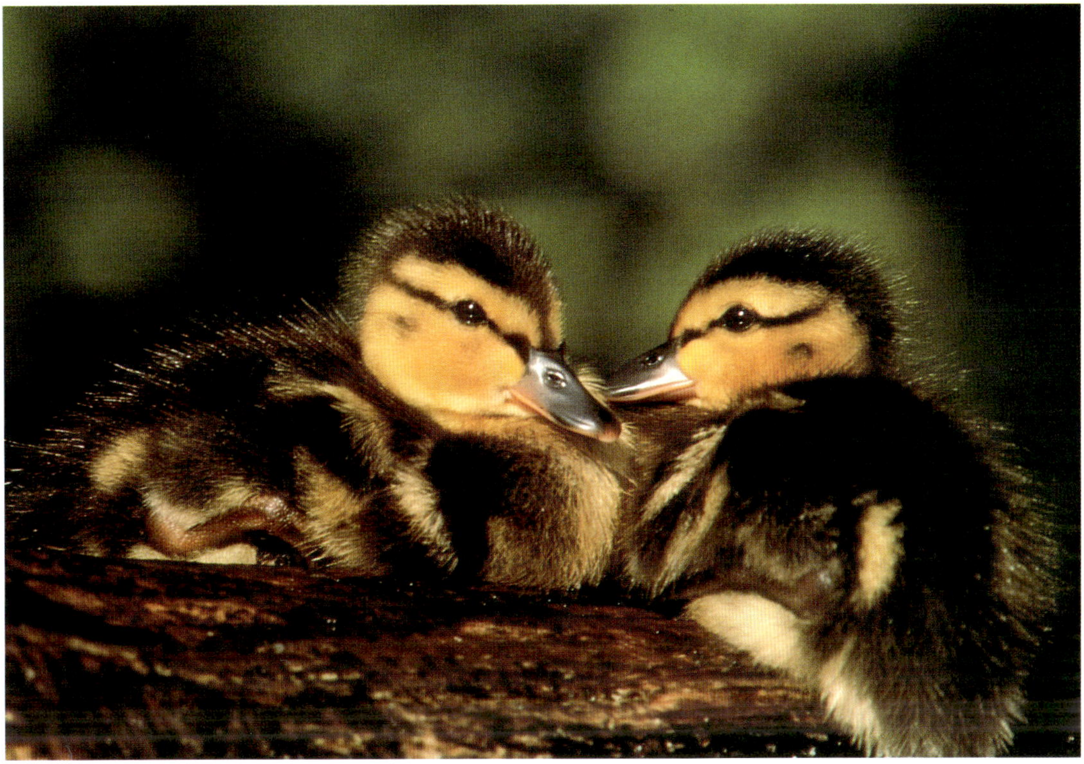

Kisses are almost totally silent

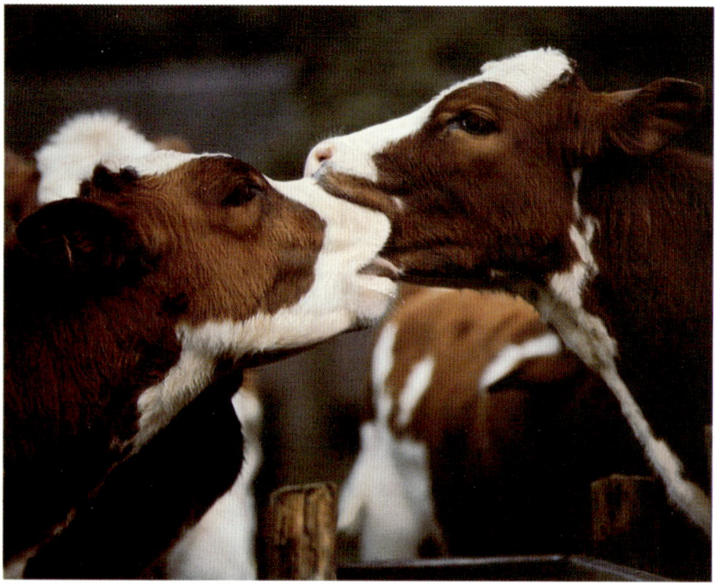

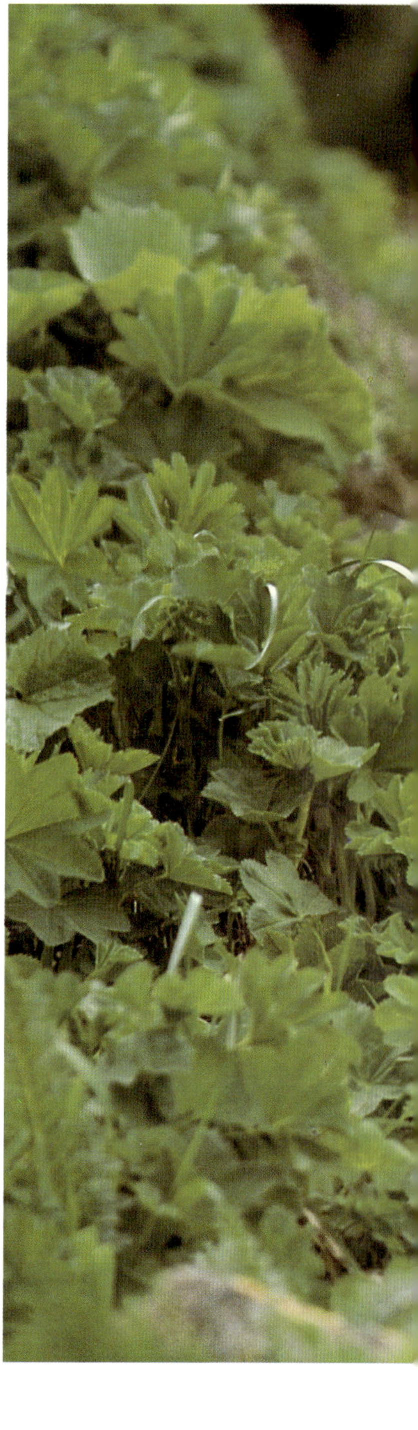

"Give me a thousand kisses."

(Catullus)

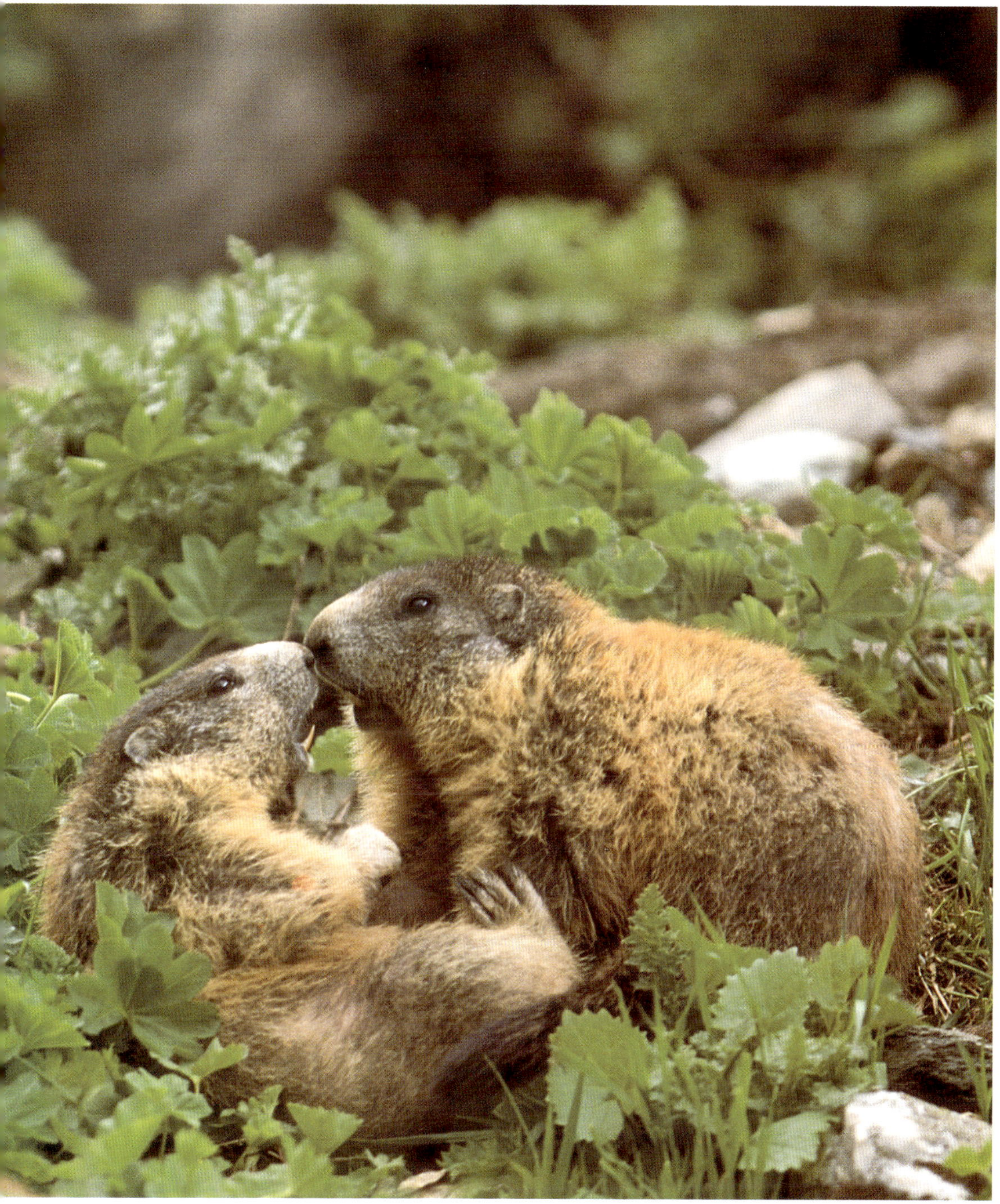

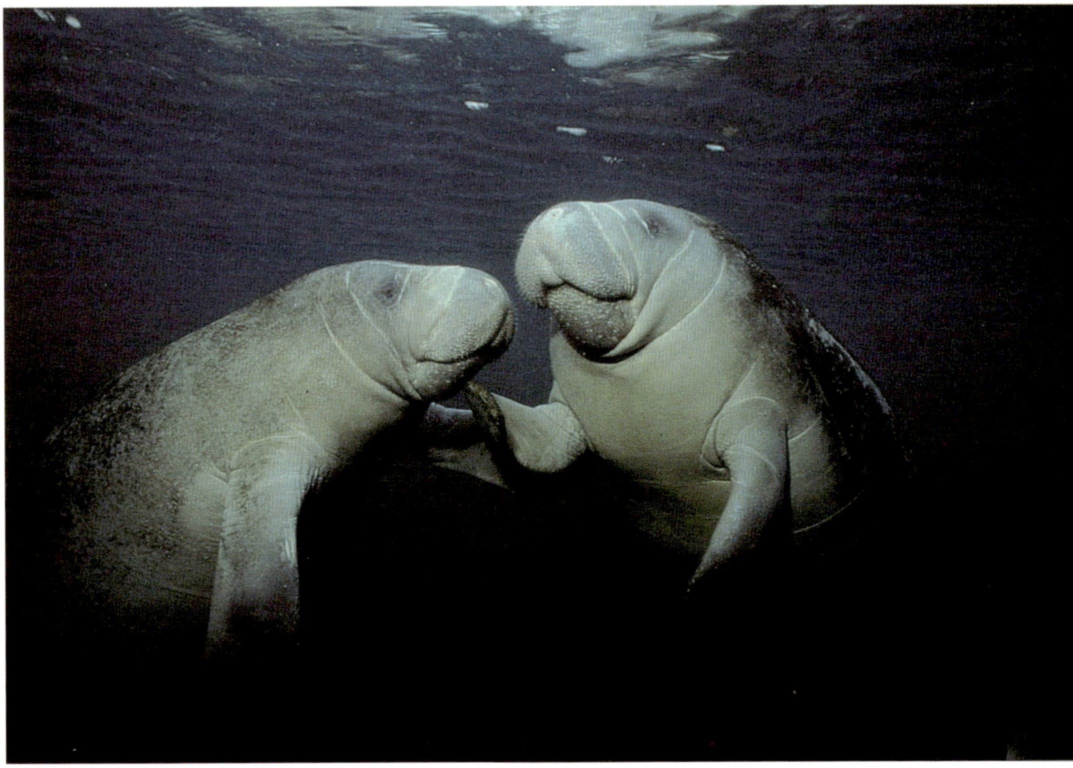

"Every kiss cries out for another. Ah!"

(Marcel Proust)

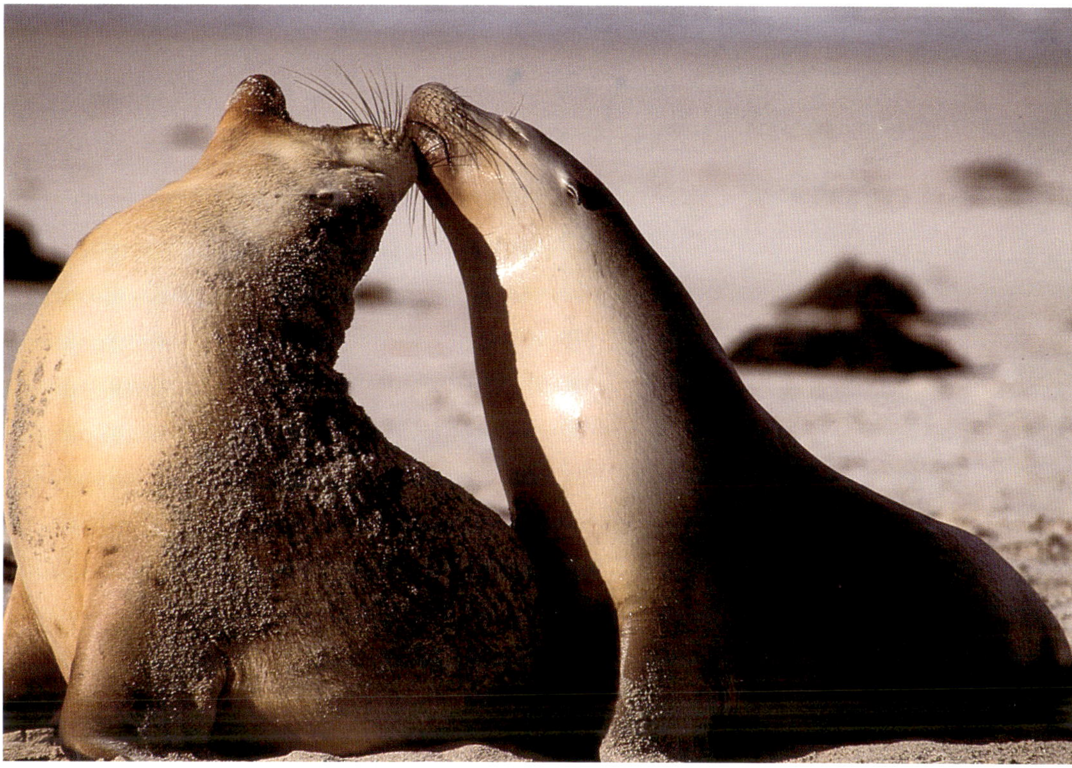

Seal it with a kiss

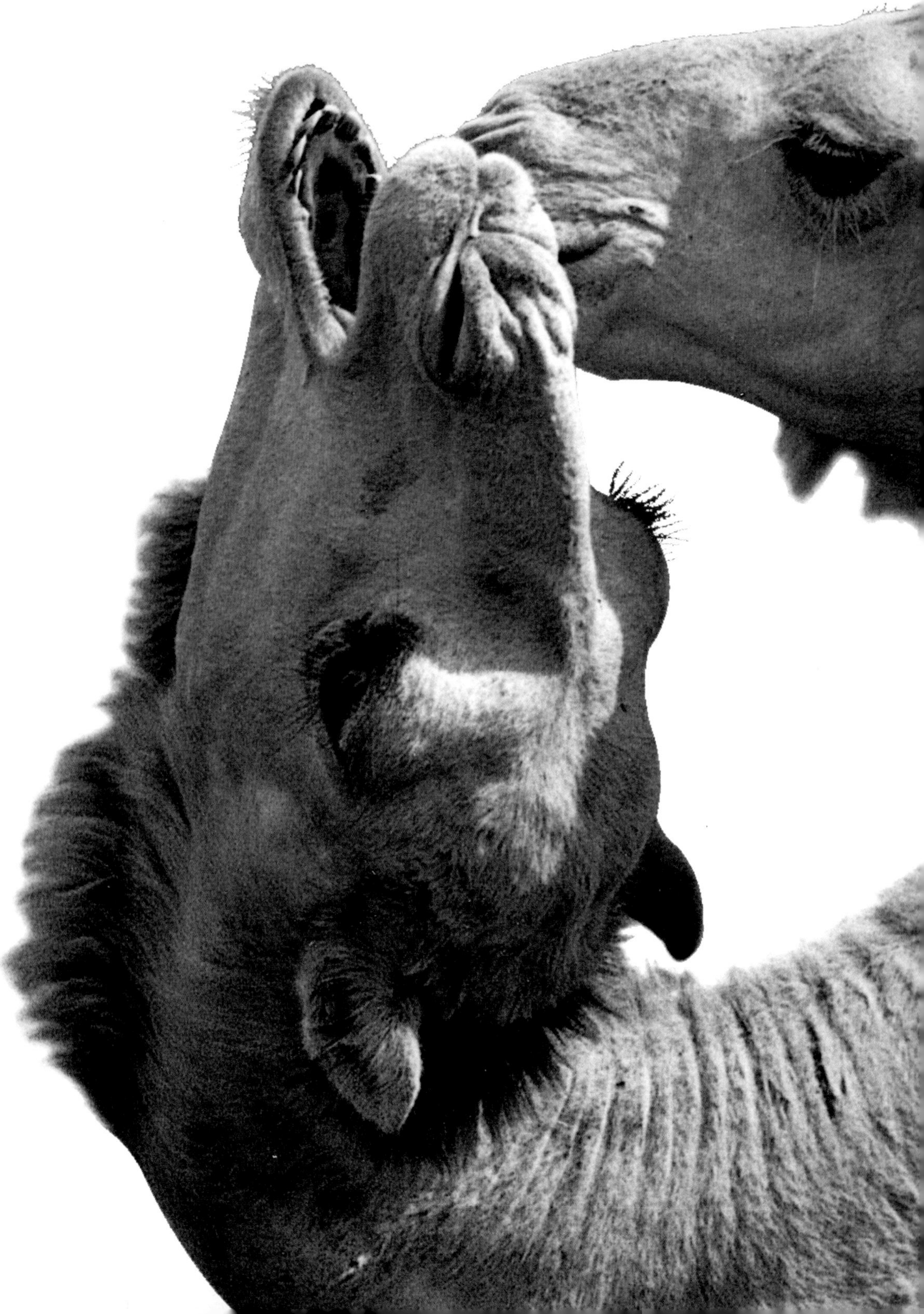

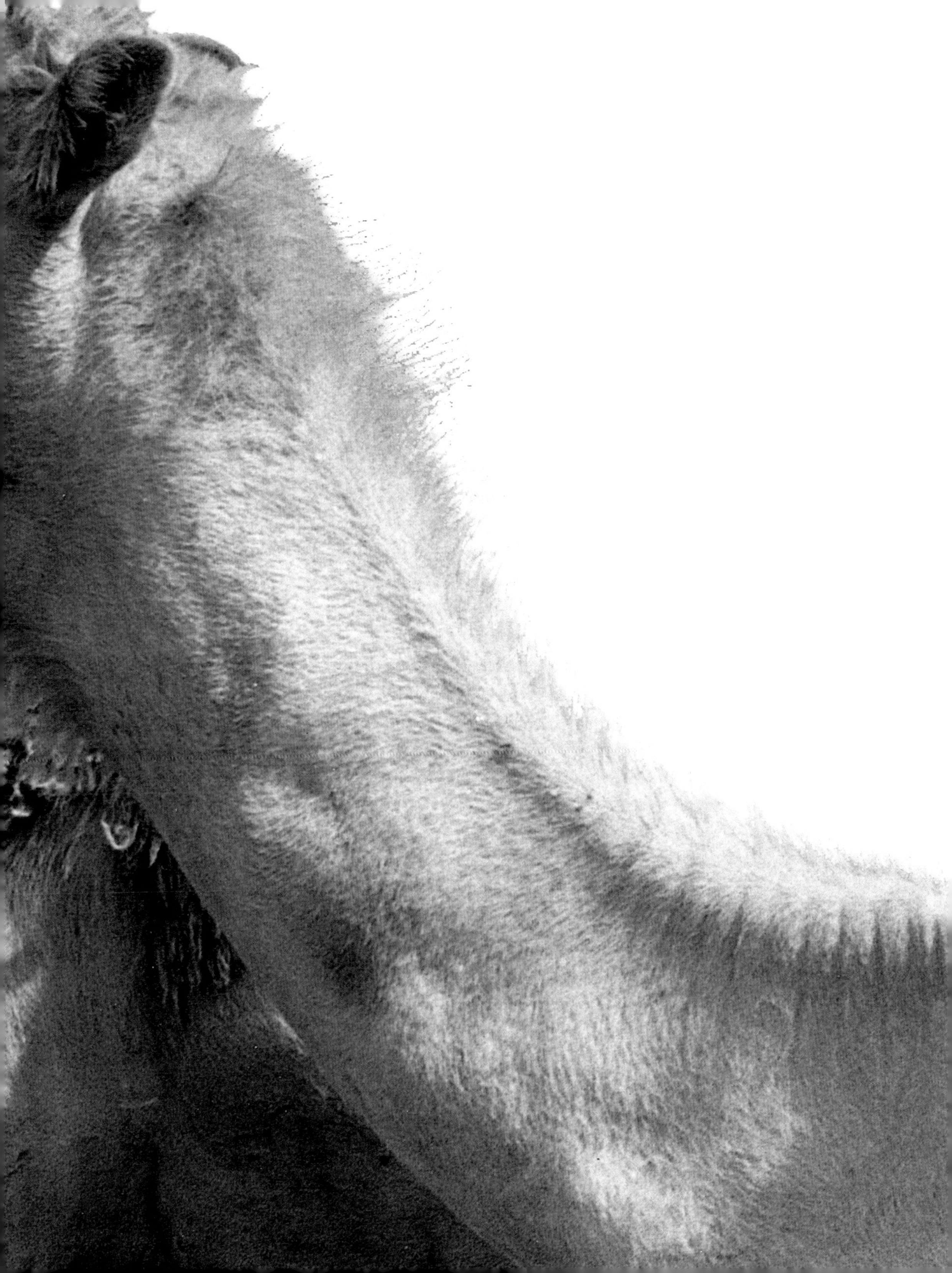

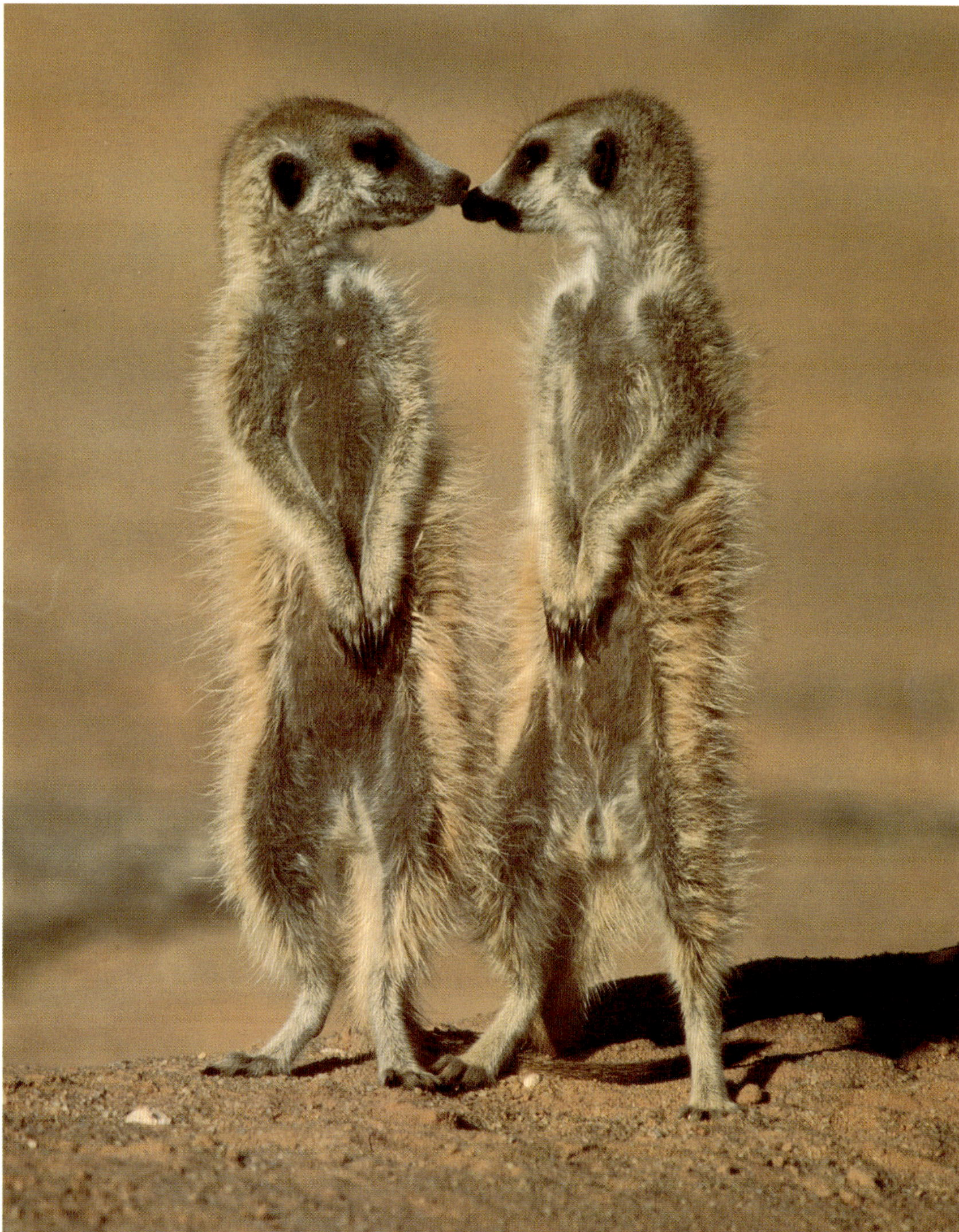

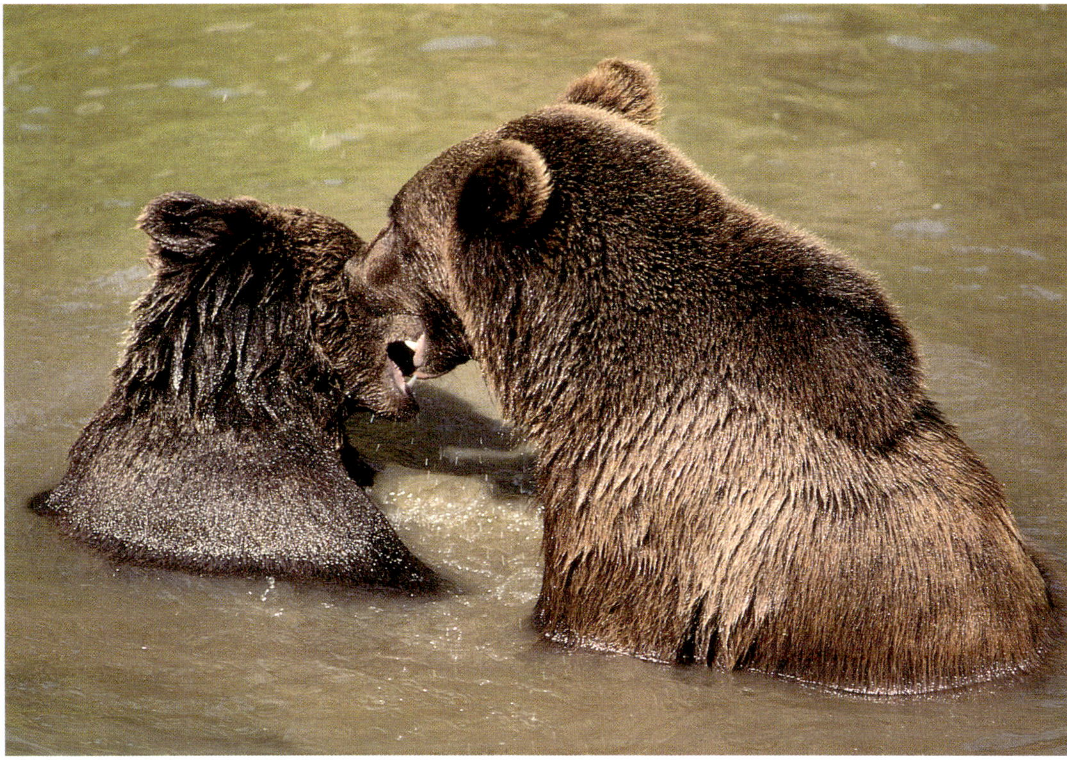

"I understand thy kisses, and thou mine,
And that's a feeling disputation."

(William Shakespeare)

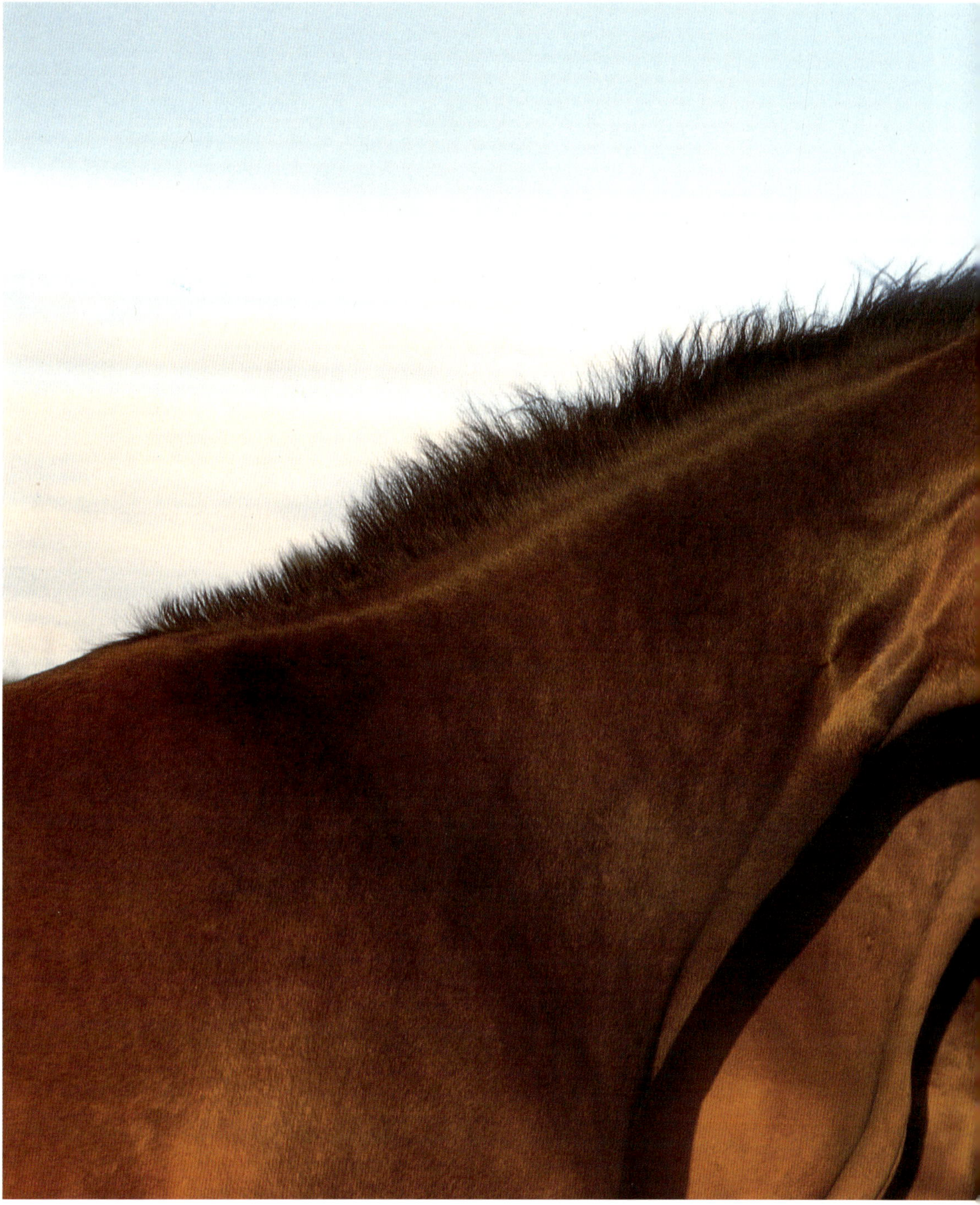

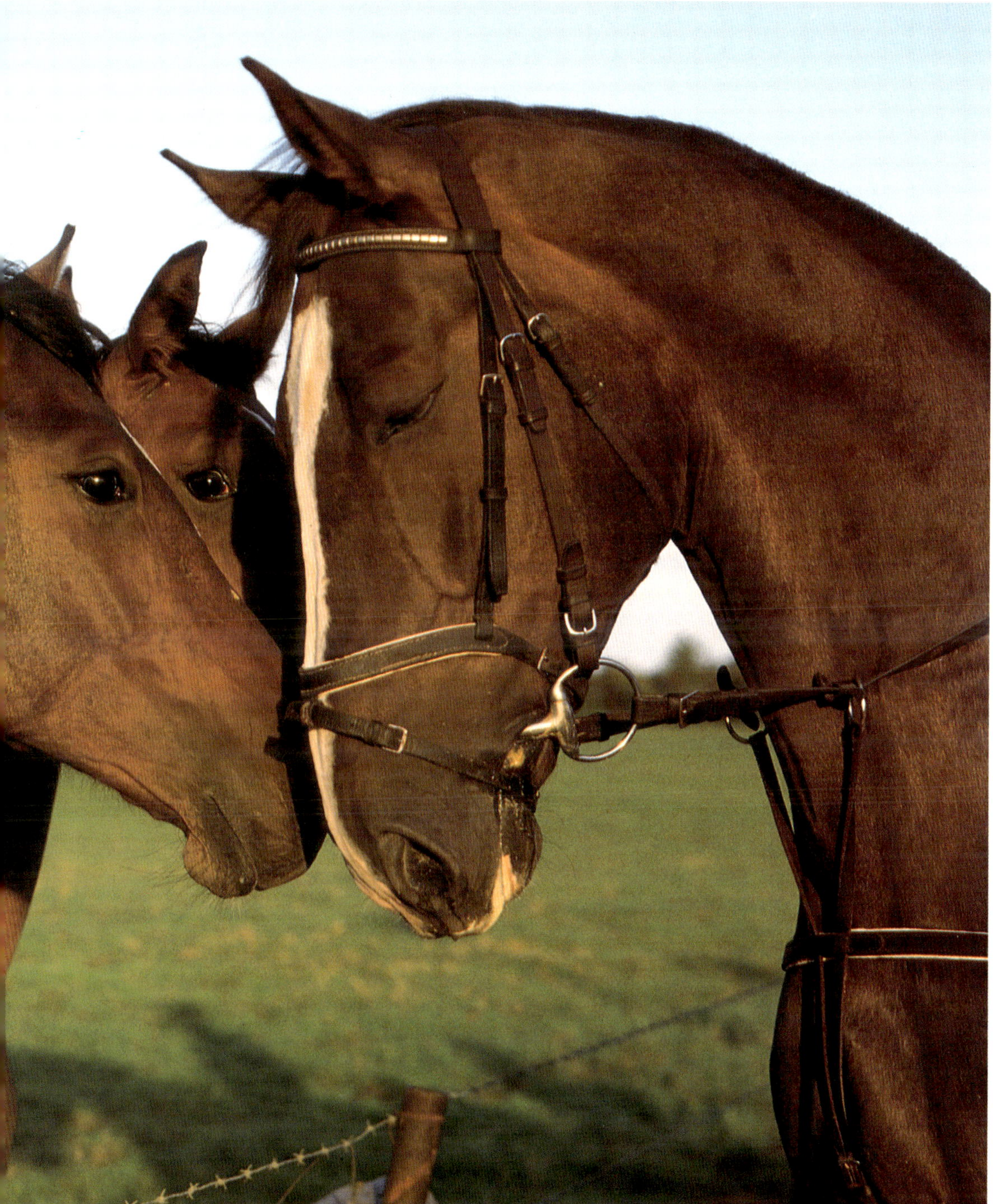

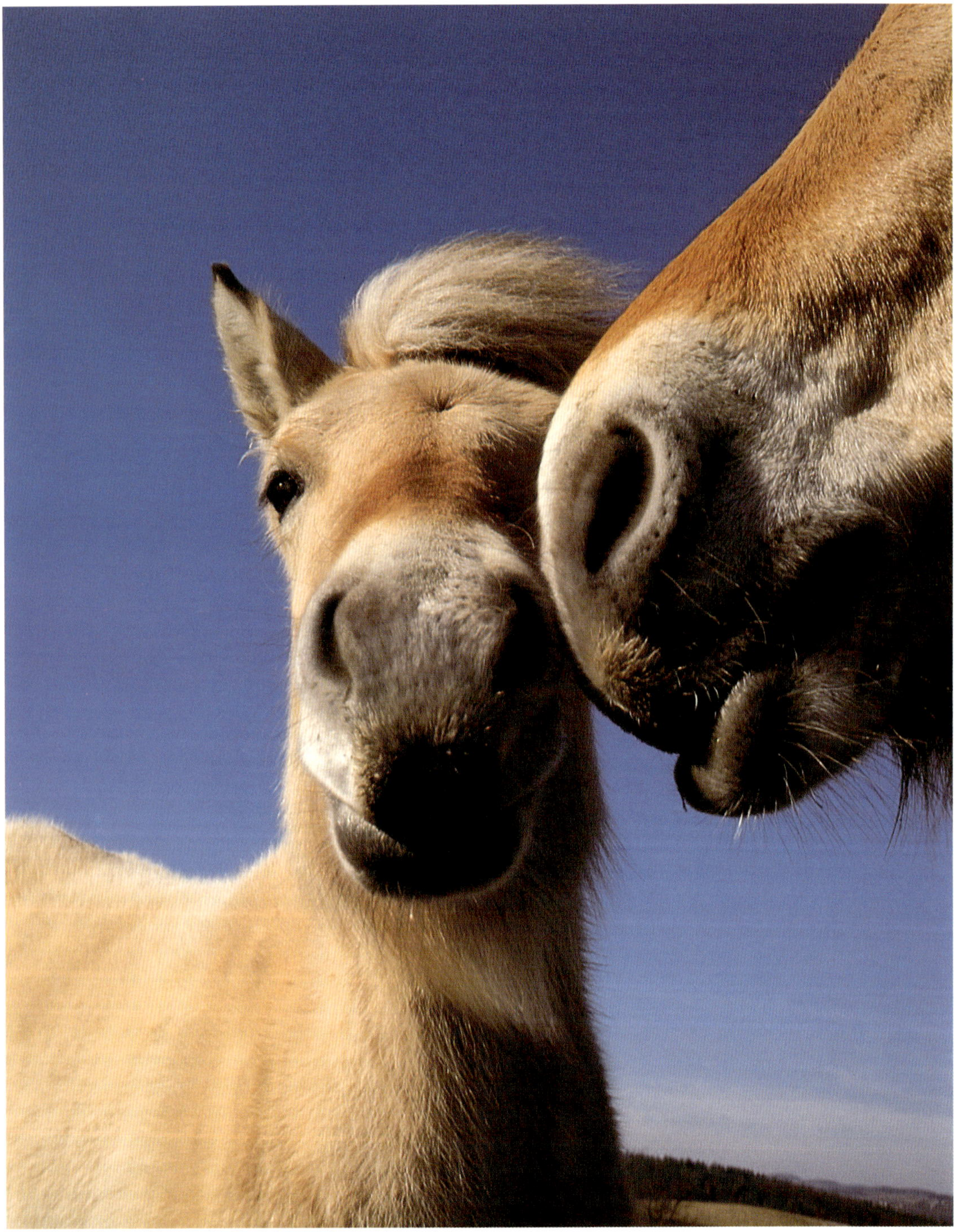

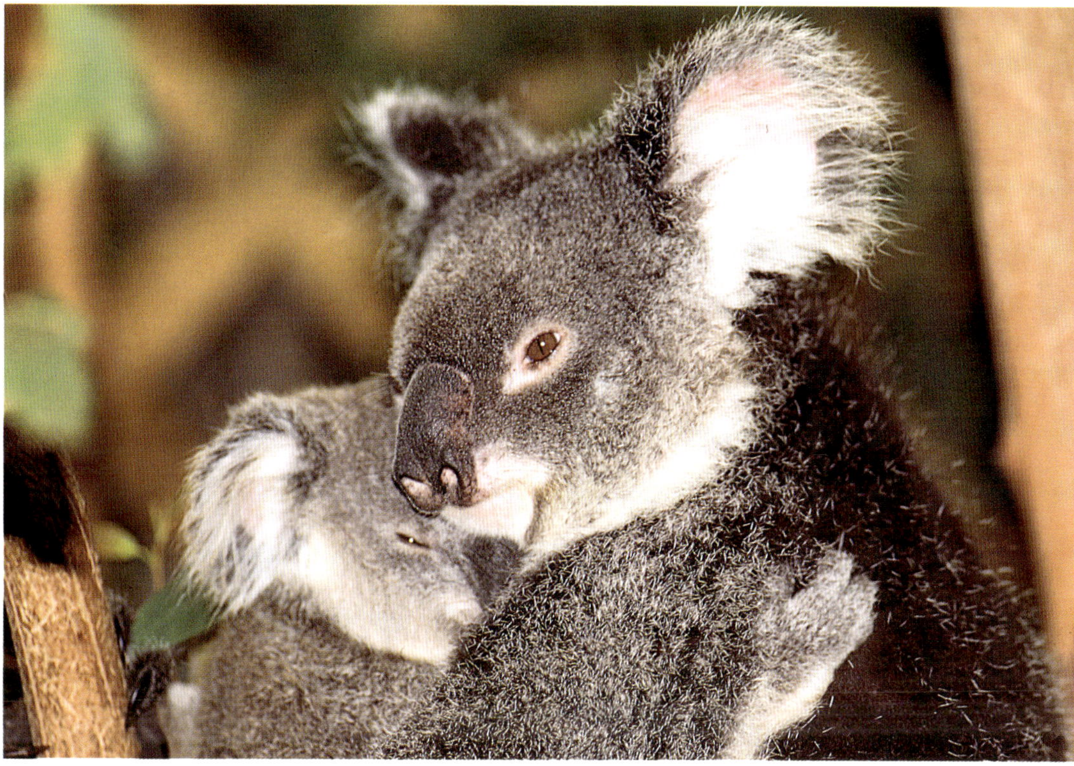

Kiss and cuddle

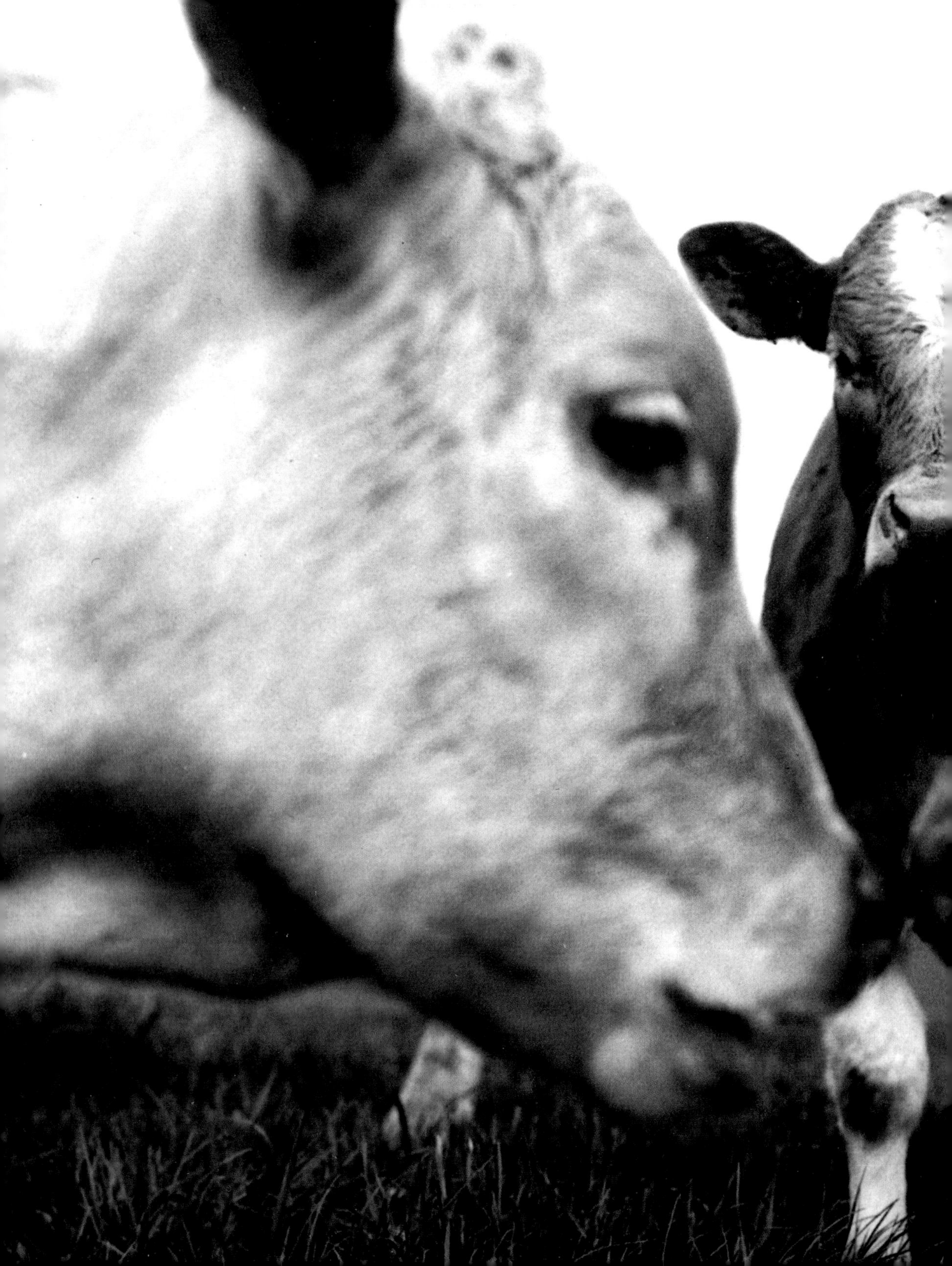

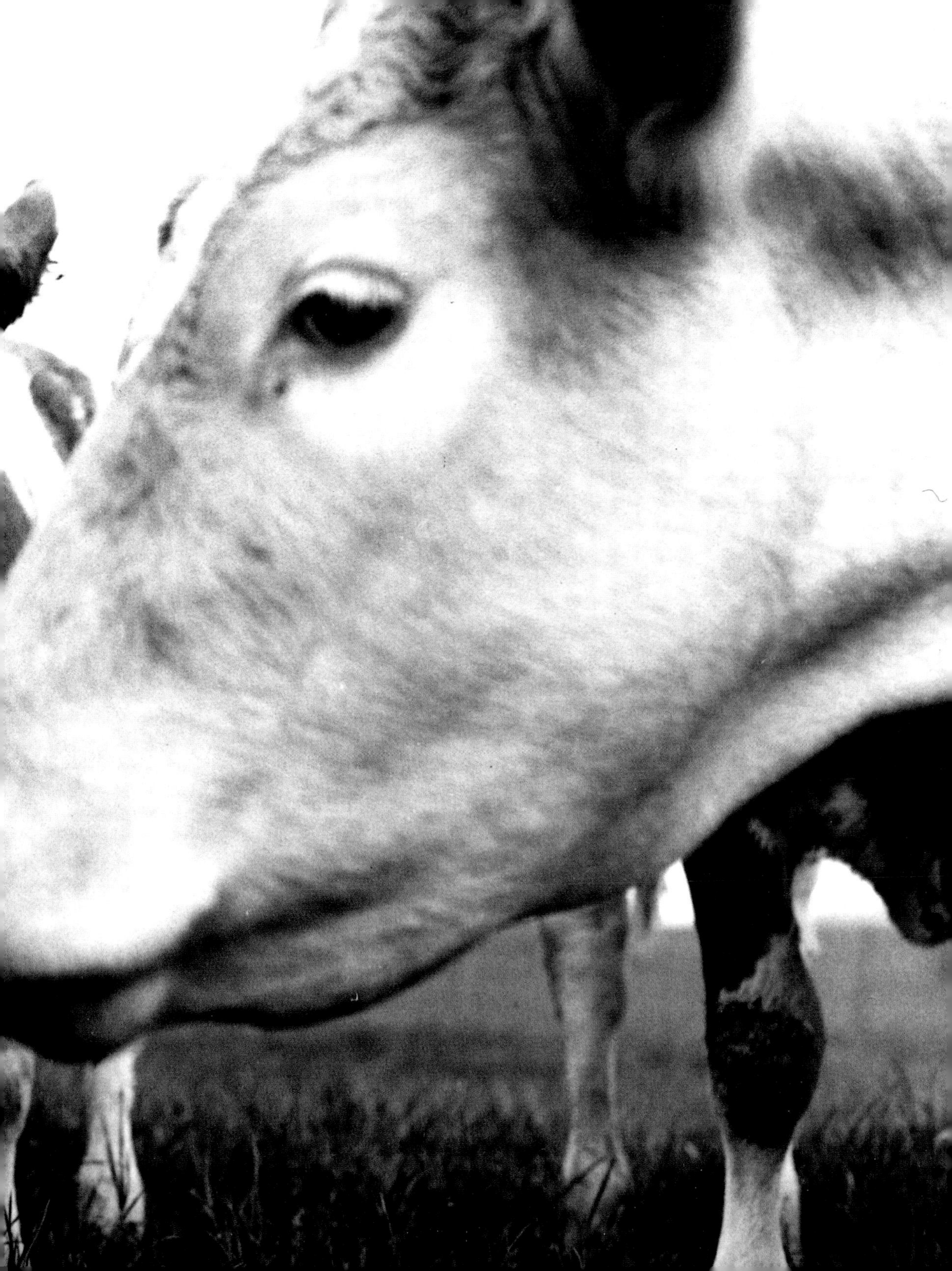

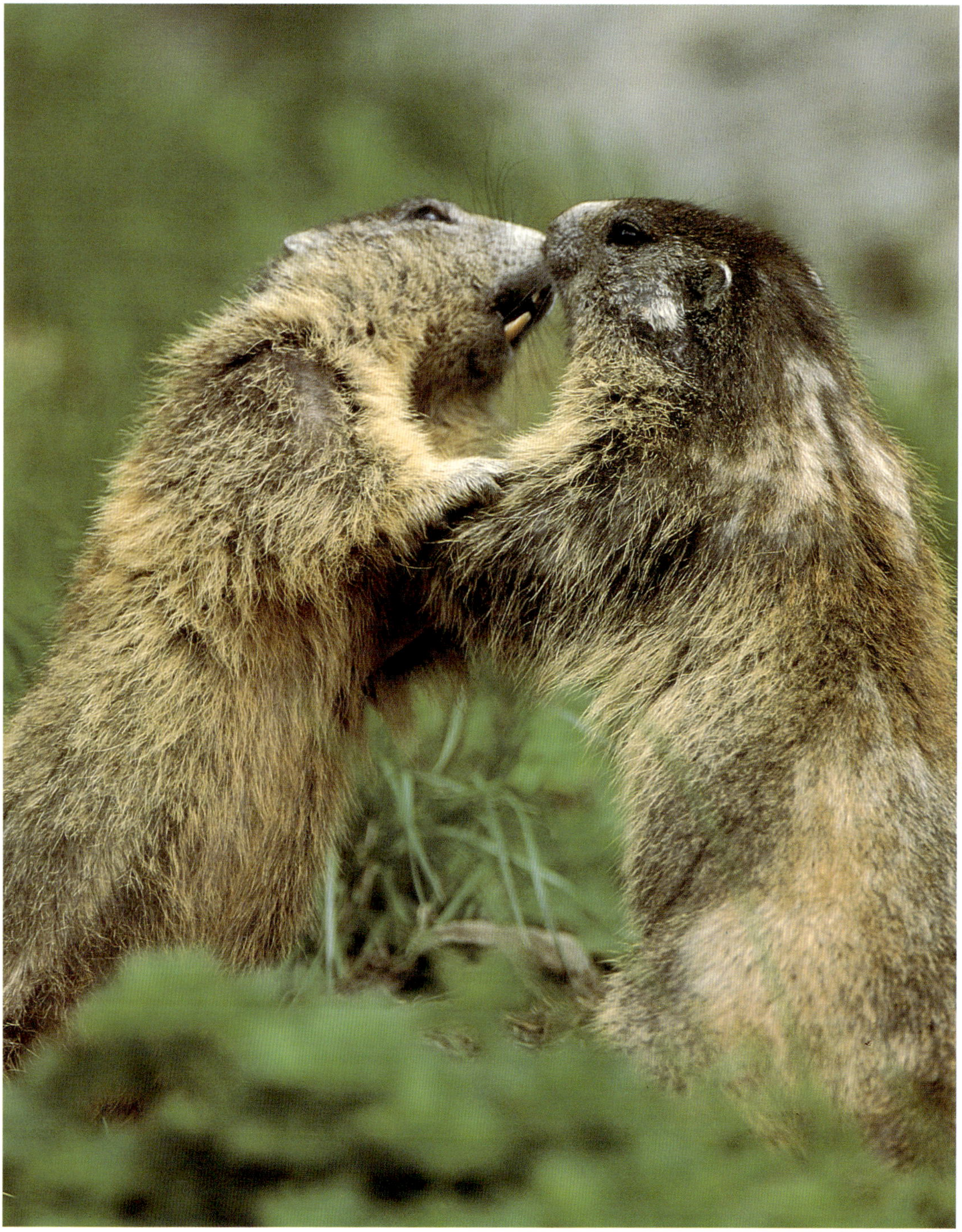

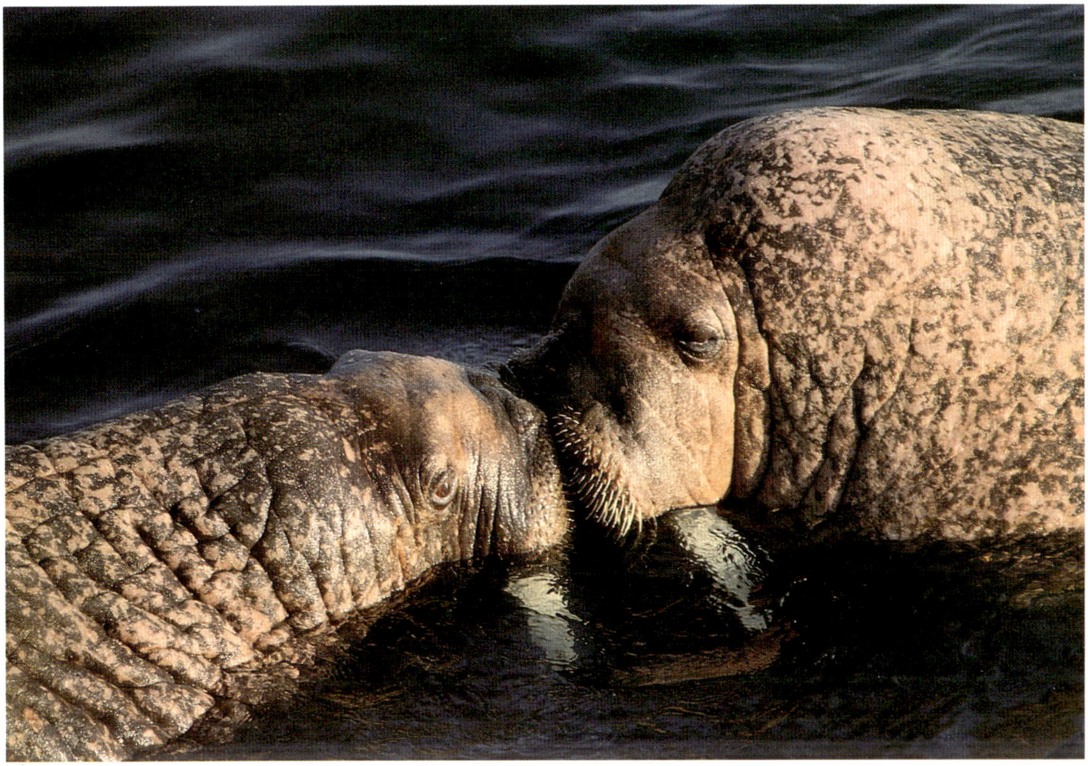

"Make me immortal with a kiss!"

(Christopher Marlowe)

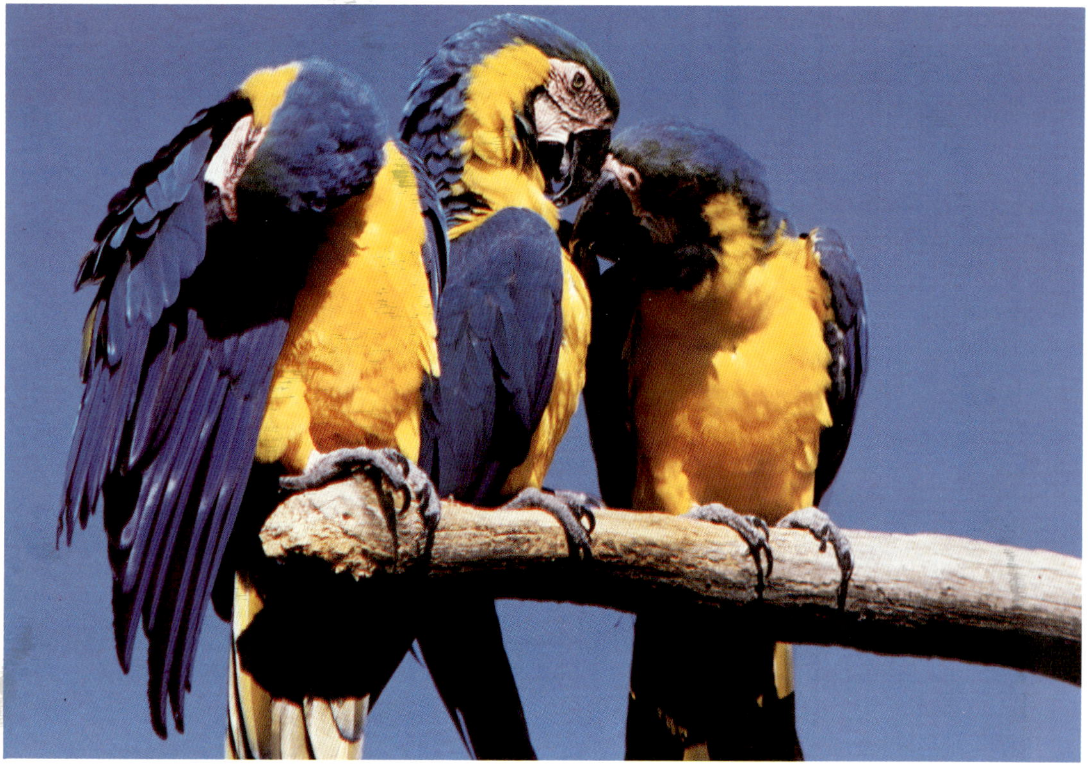

"For a glance, a world; for a smile, a heaven; for a kiss… I do not know what I would give you for a kiss!"

(Gustavo Adolfo Bécquer)

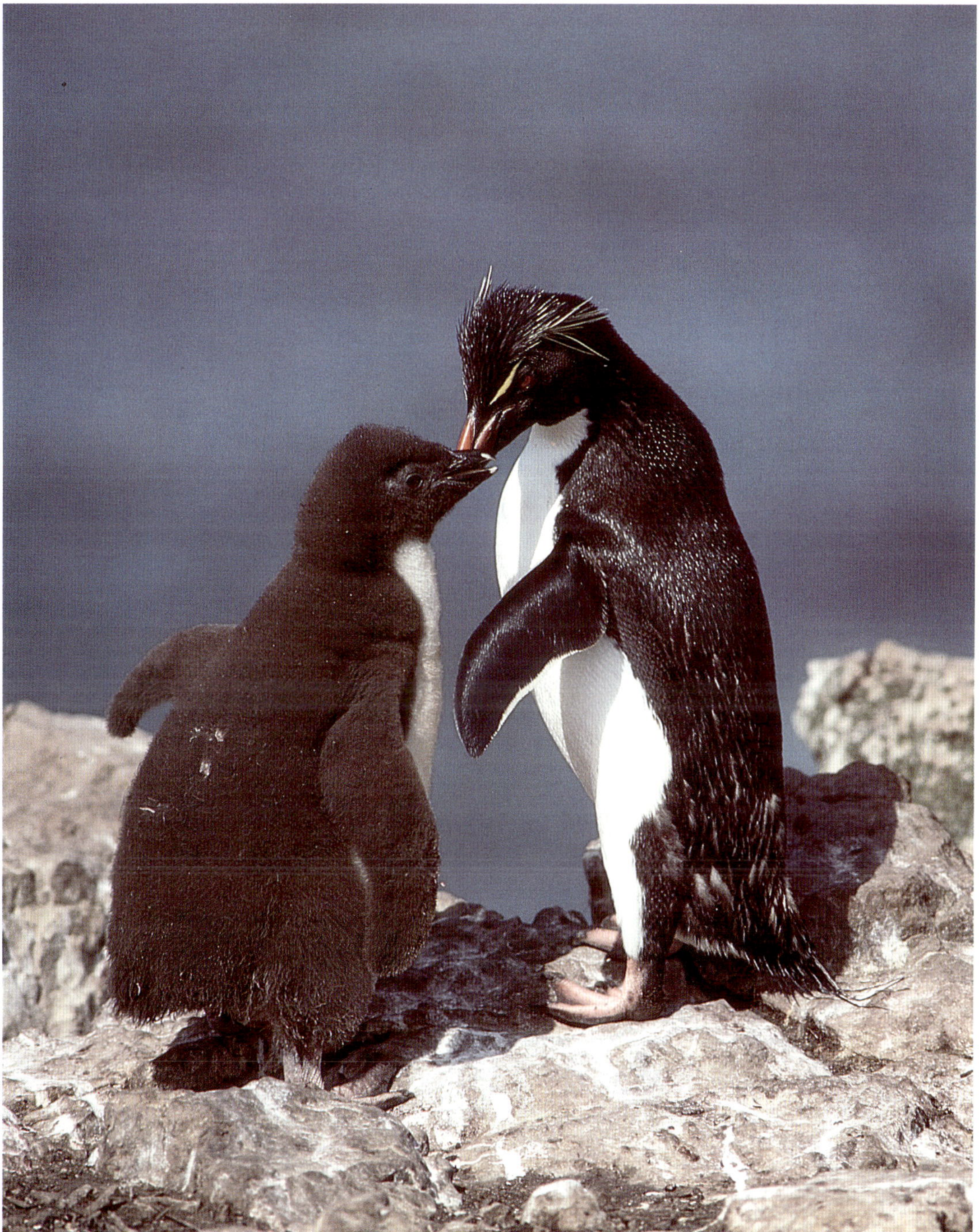

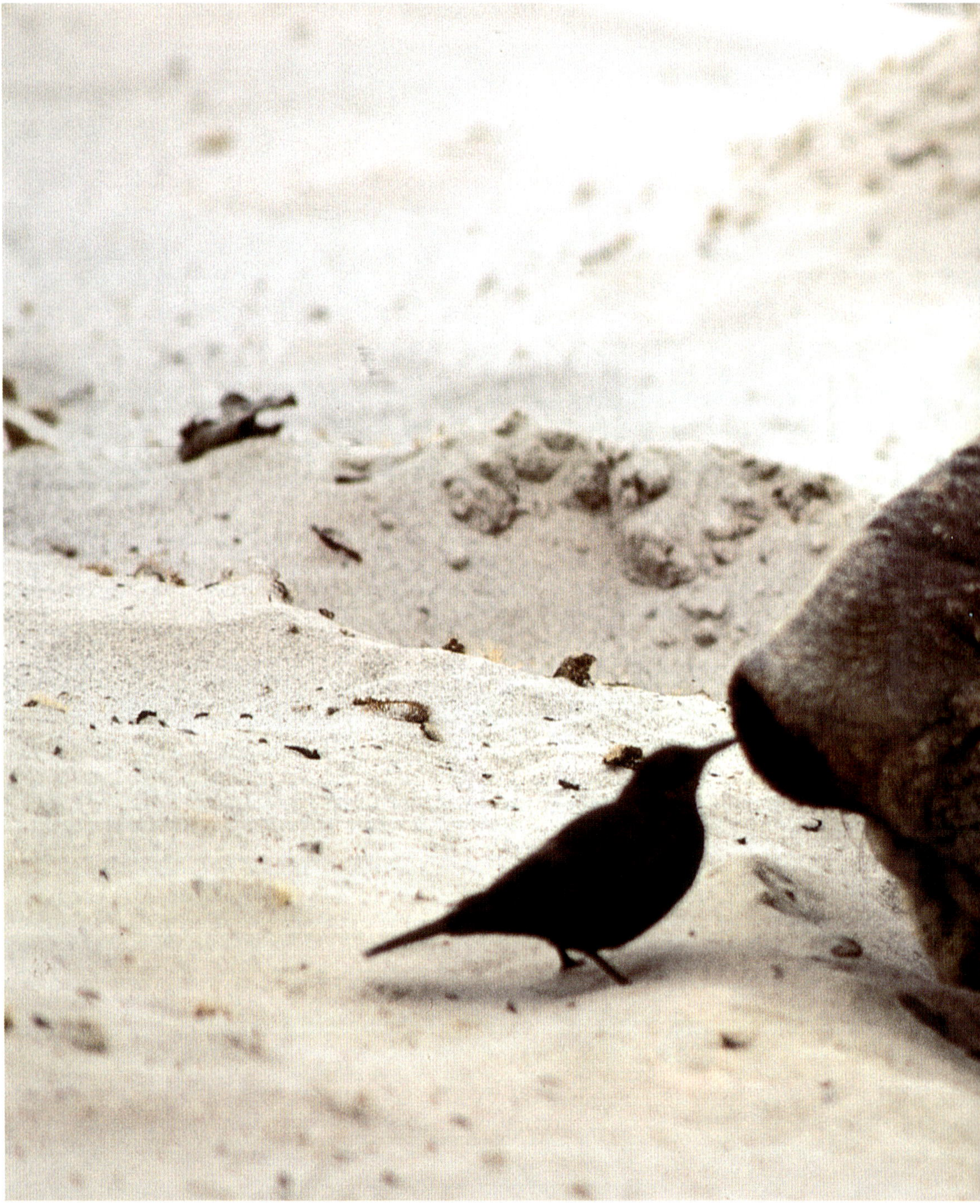

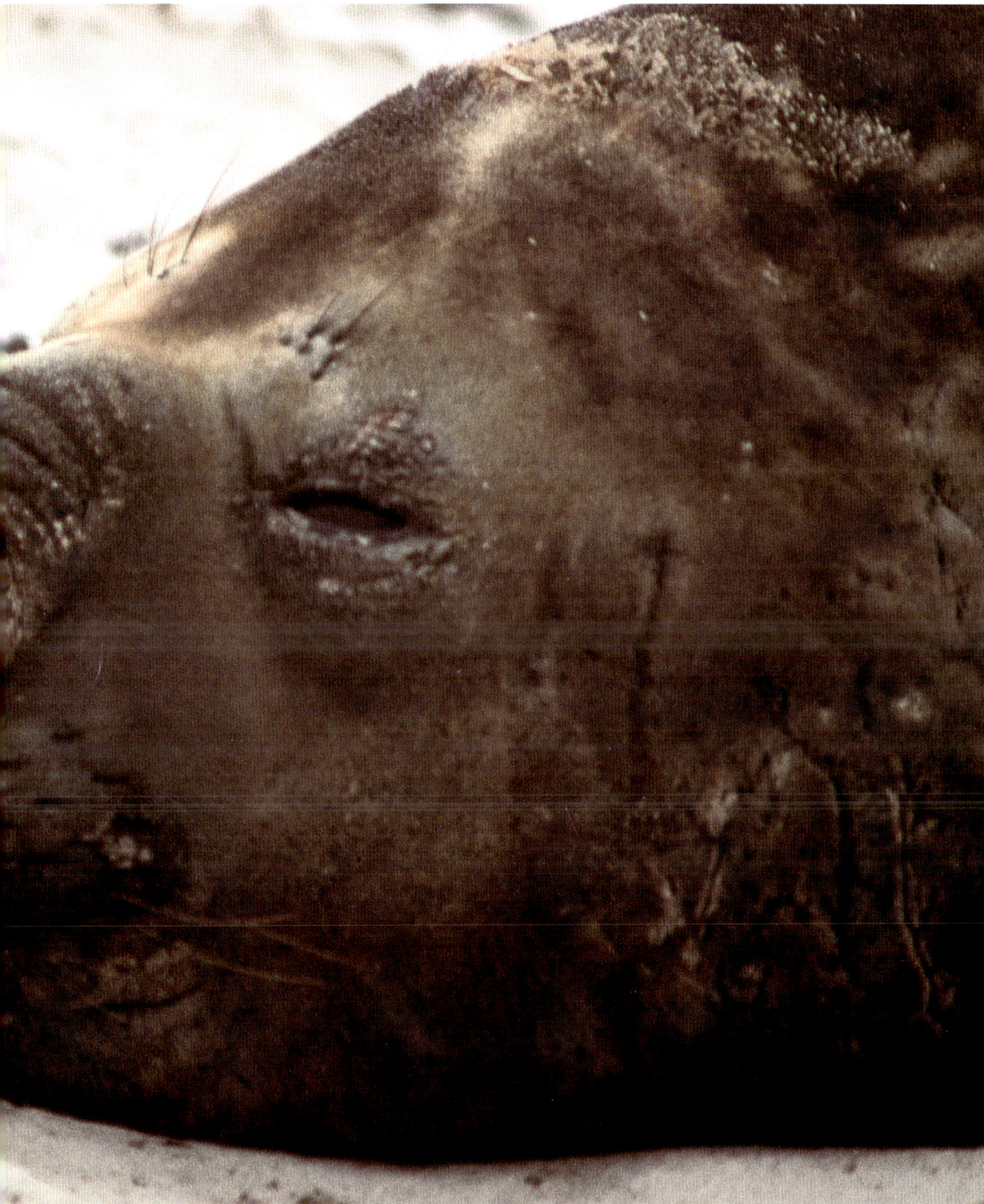

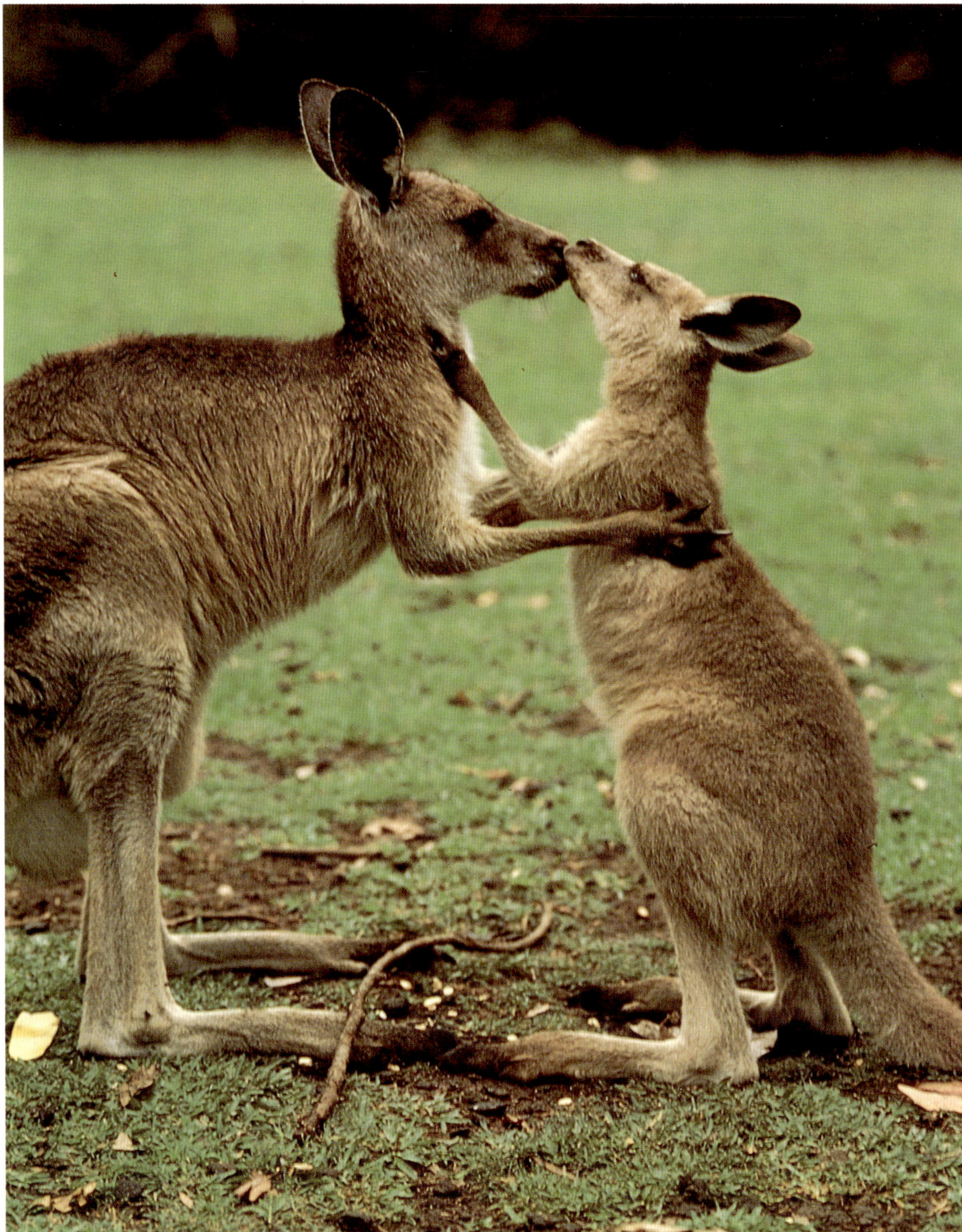

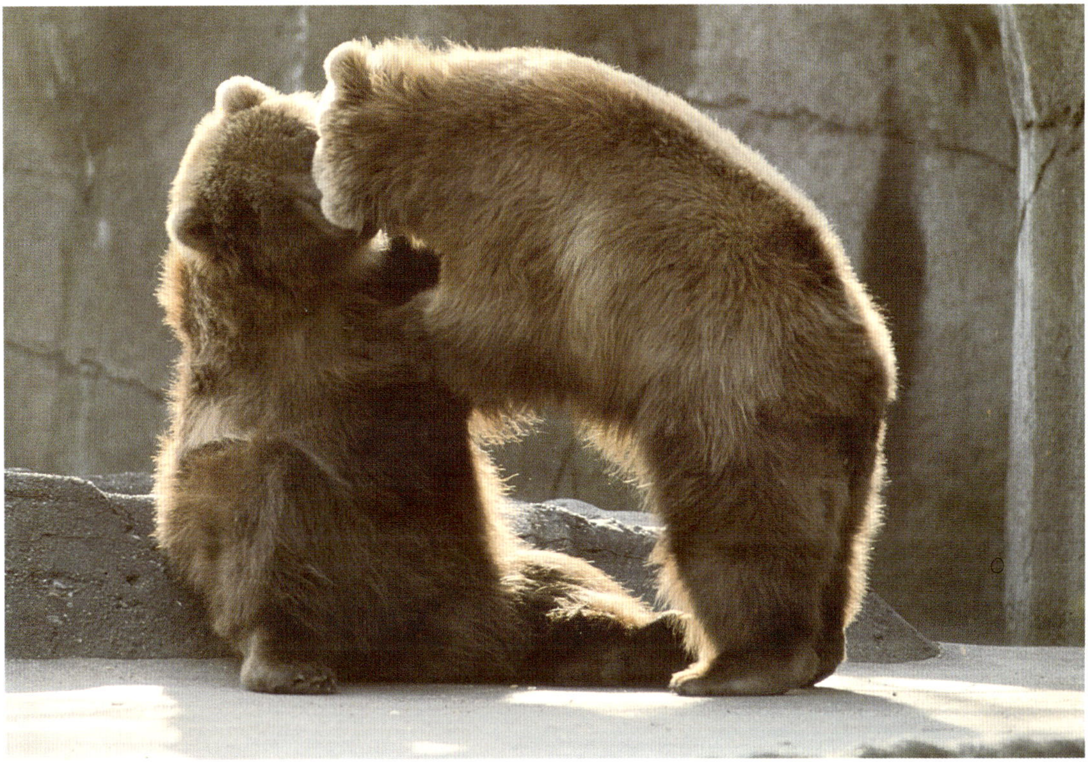

"Hold me and you will never forget me."

(Brigitte Bardot)

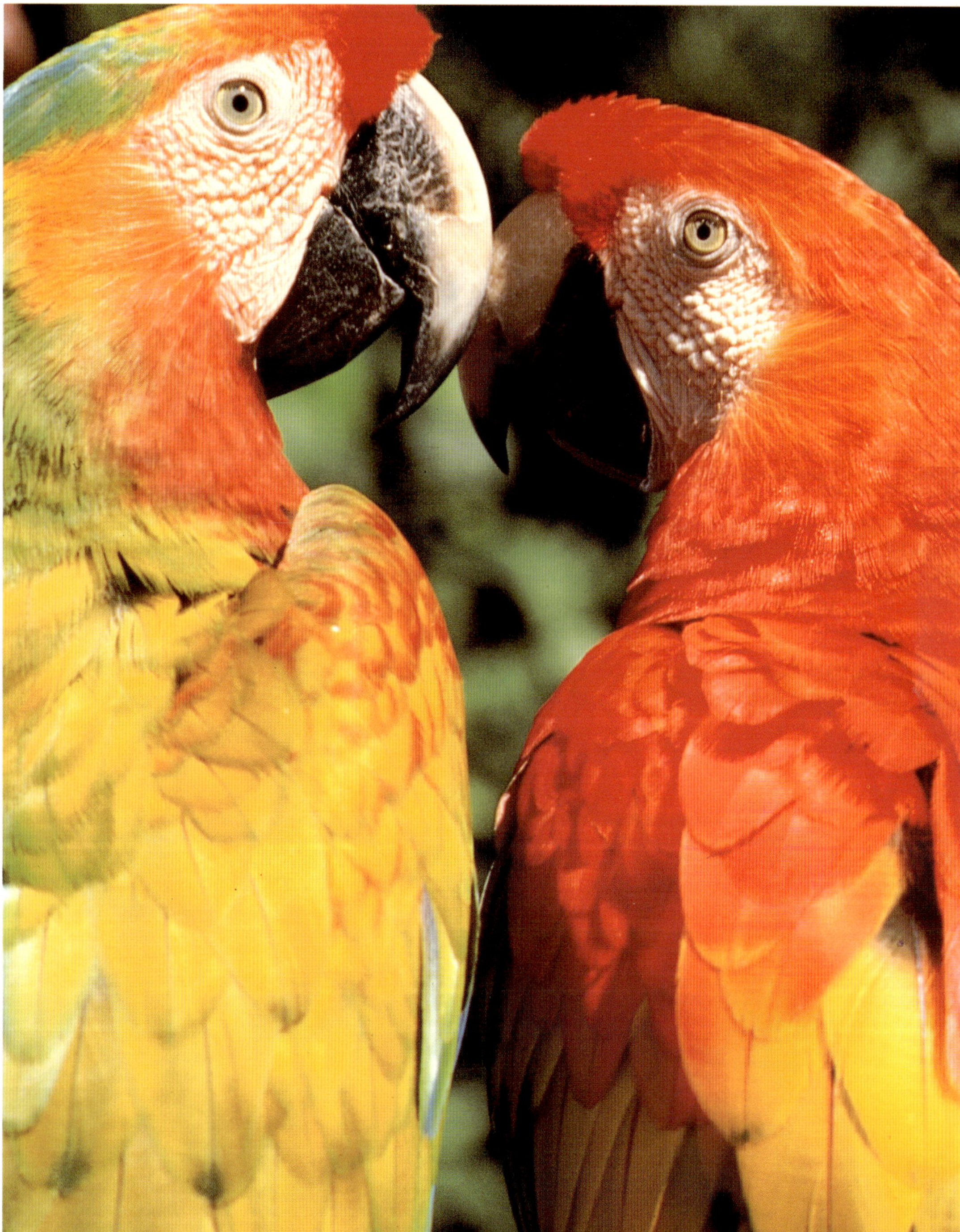

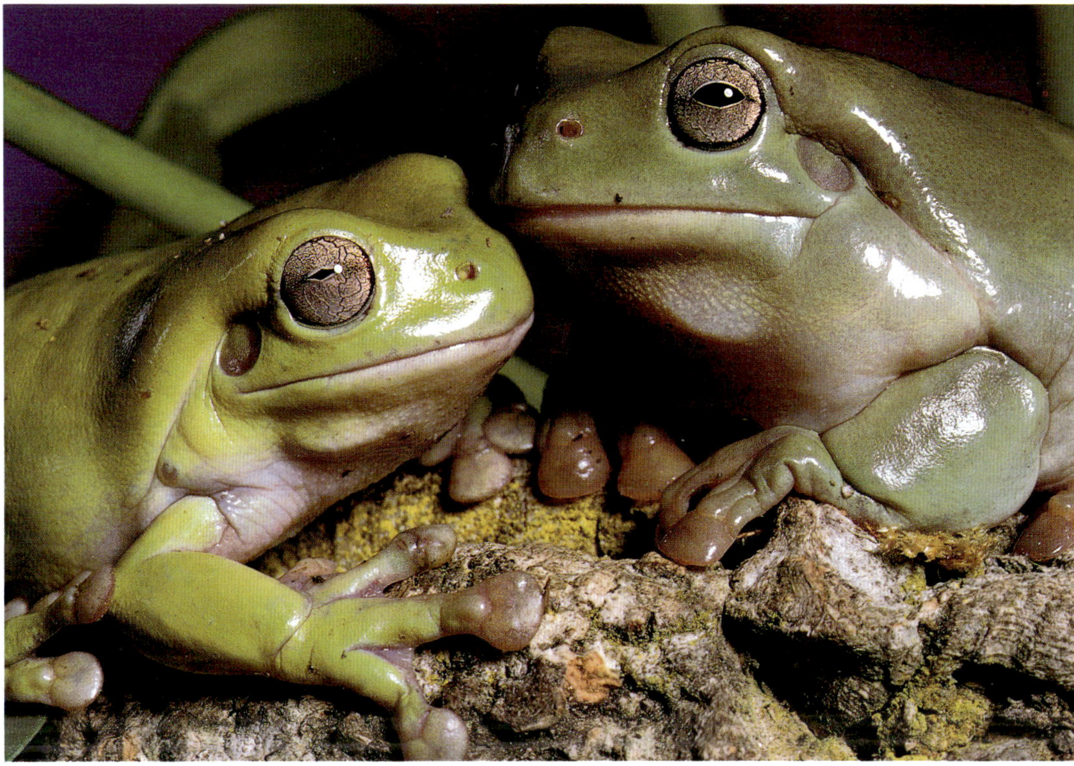

"Some of 'em want to be kissed and some want you to talk politics... but the principle's the same."

(Harley Granville Barker)

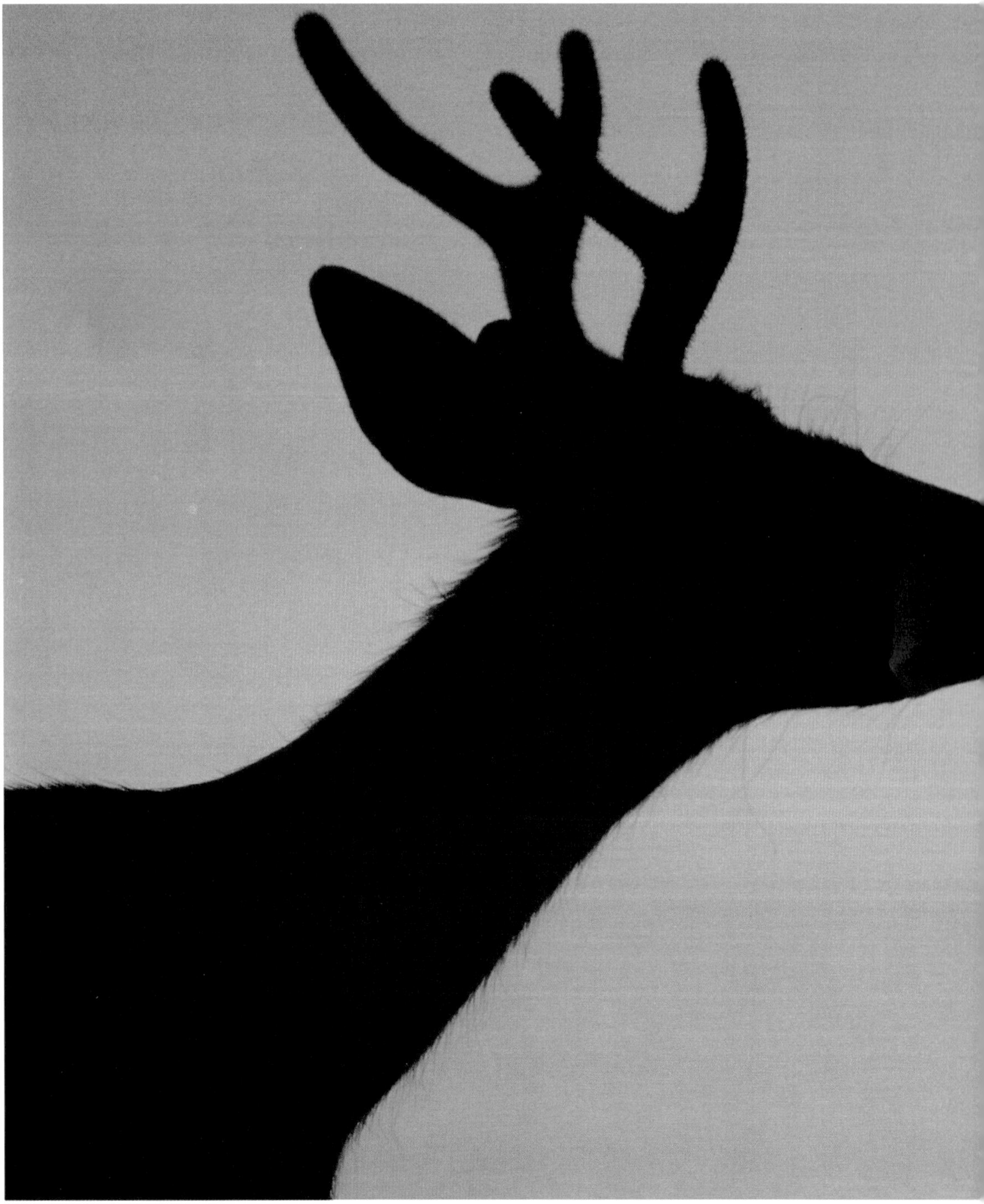

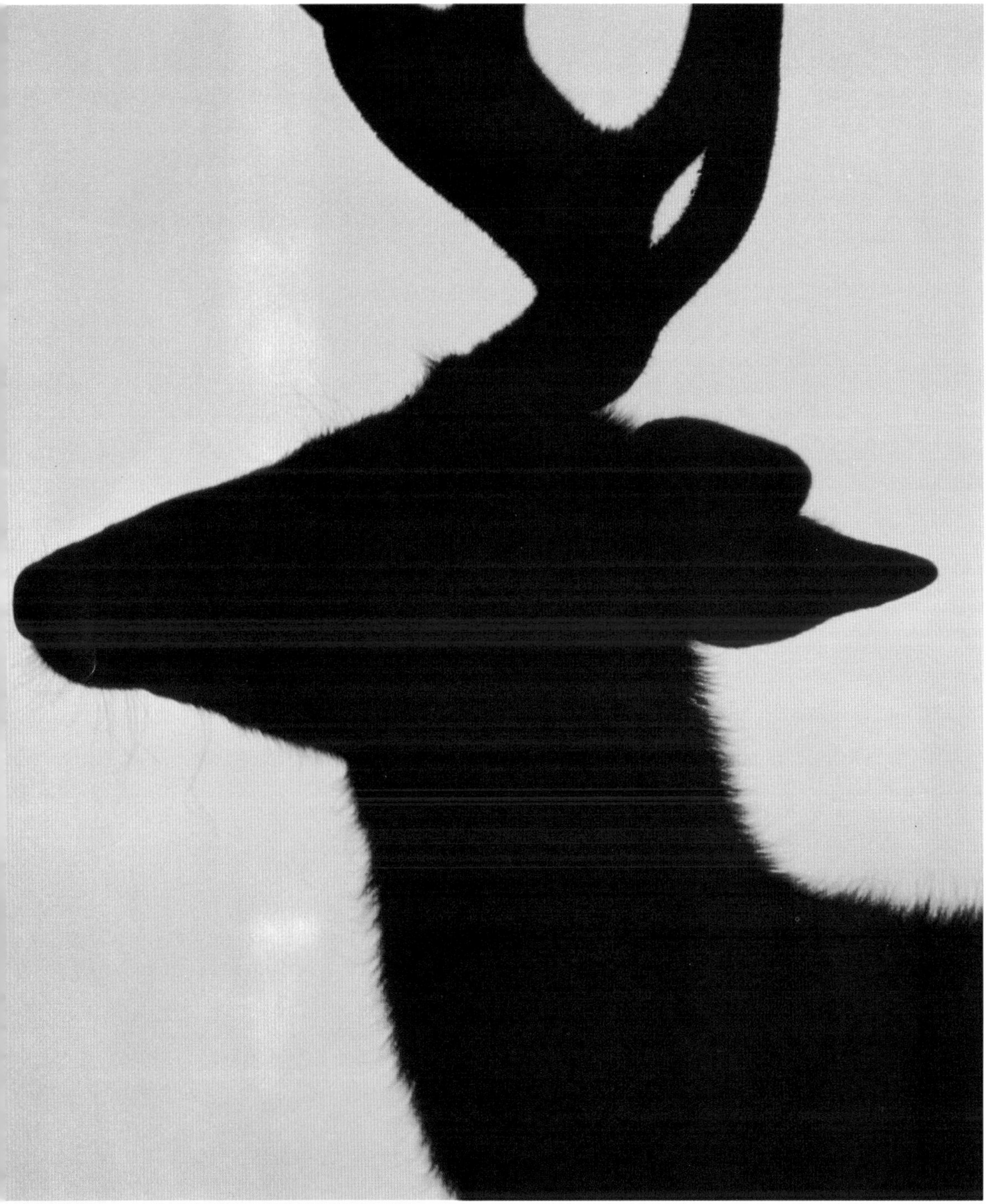

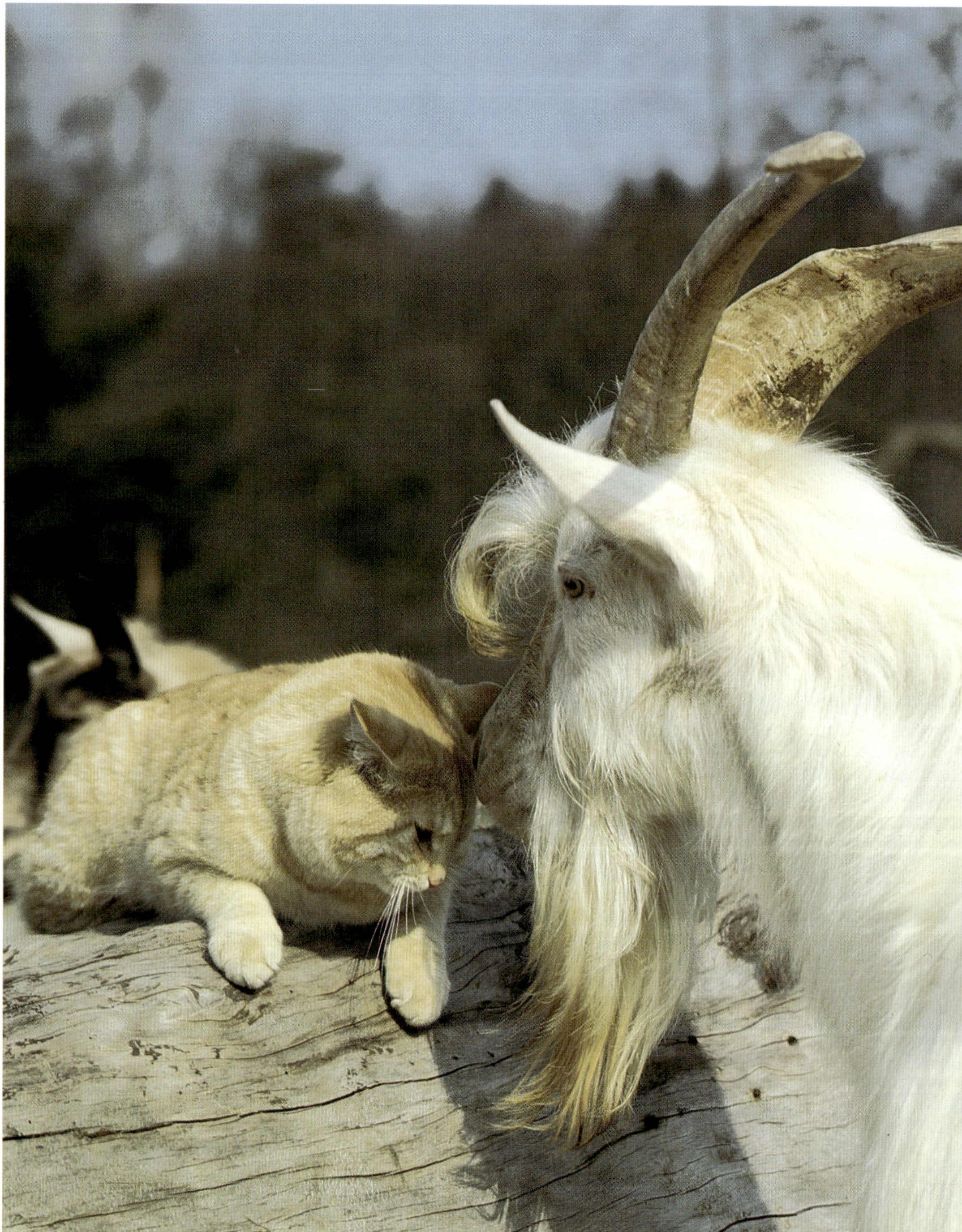

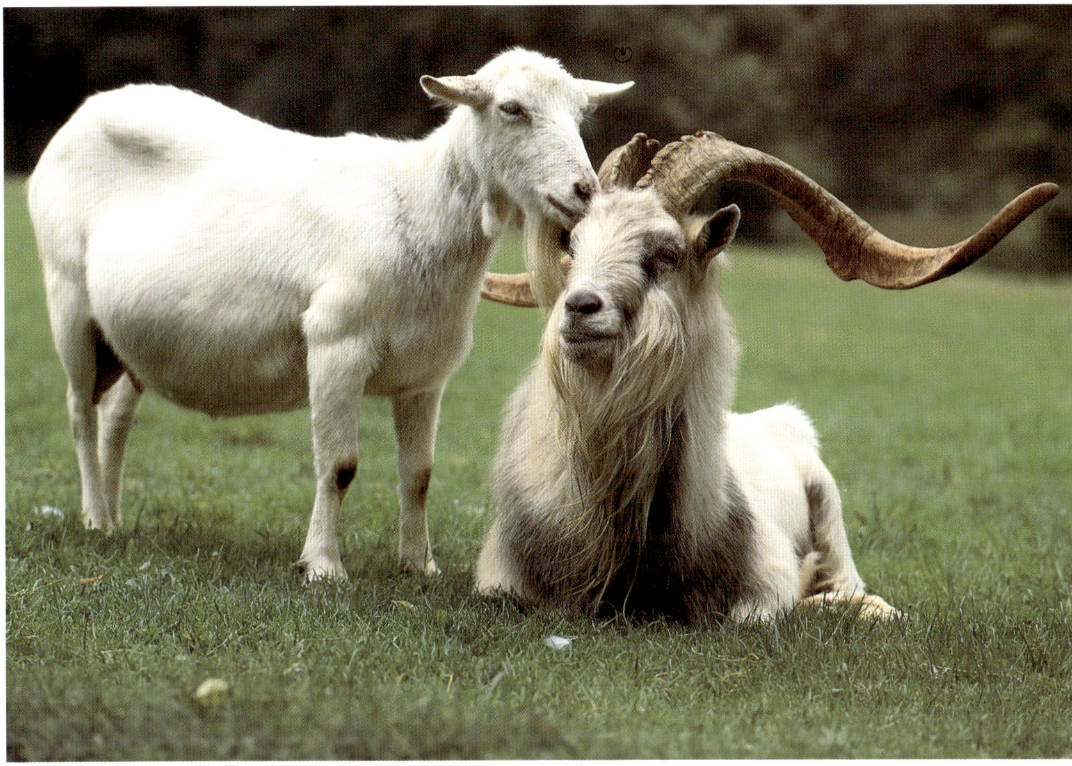

Kiss and tell

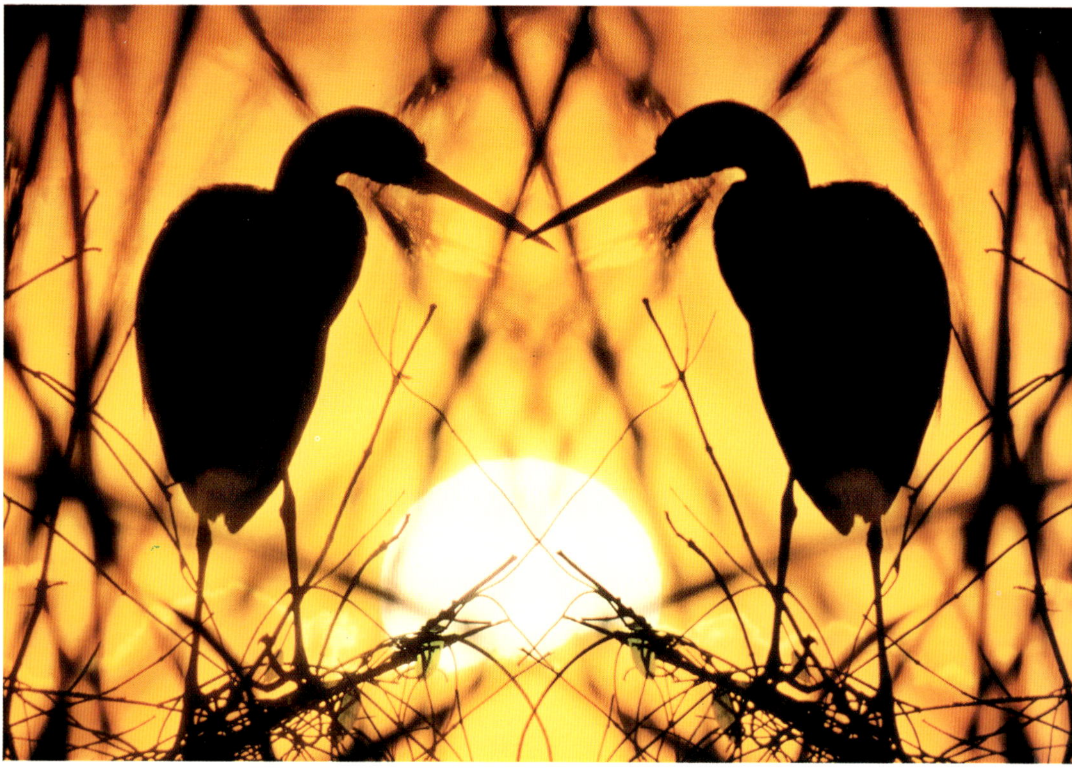

"Kisses are for the shadows, but at night they shine like the stars."

(Rémy de Gourmont)

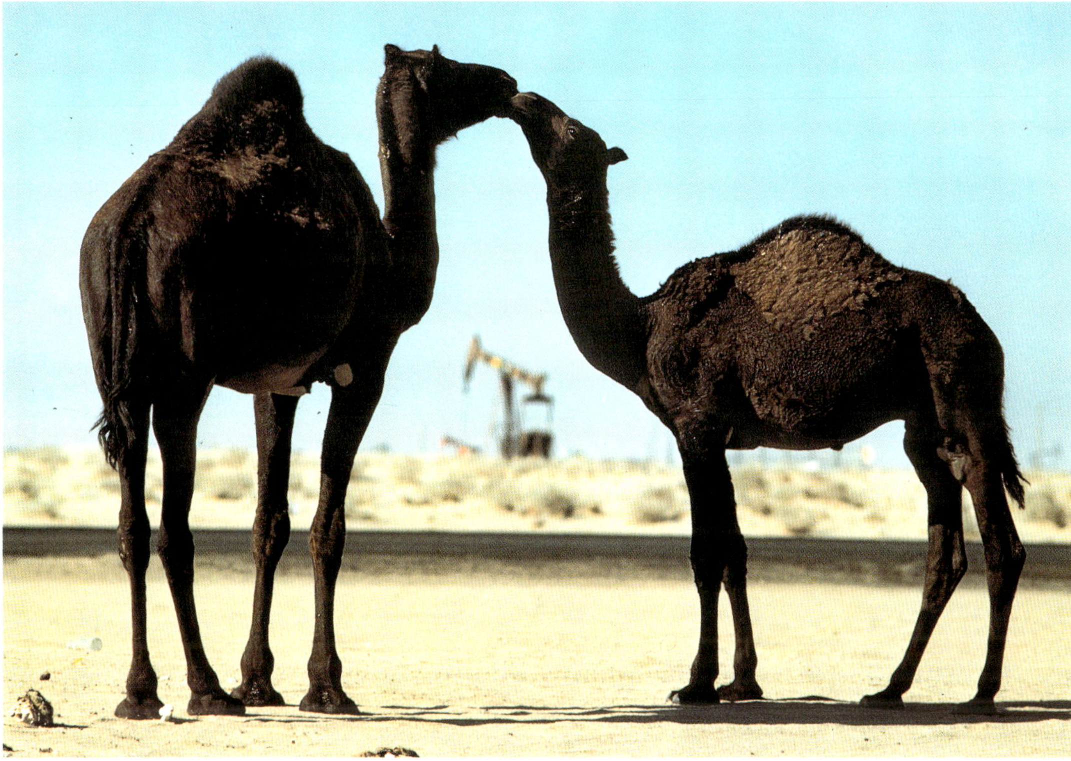

"Ae fond kiss, and then we sever!"

(Robert Burns)

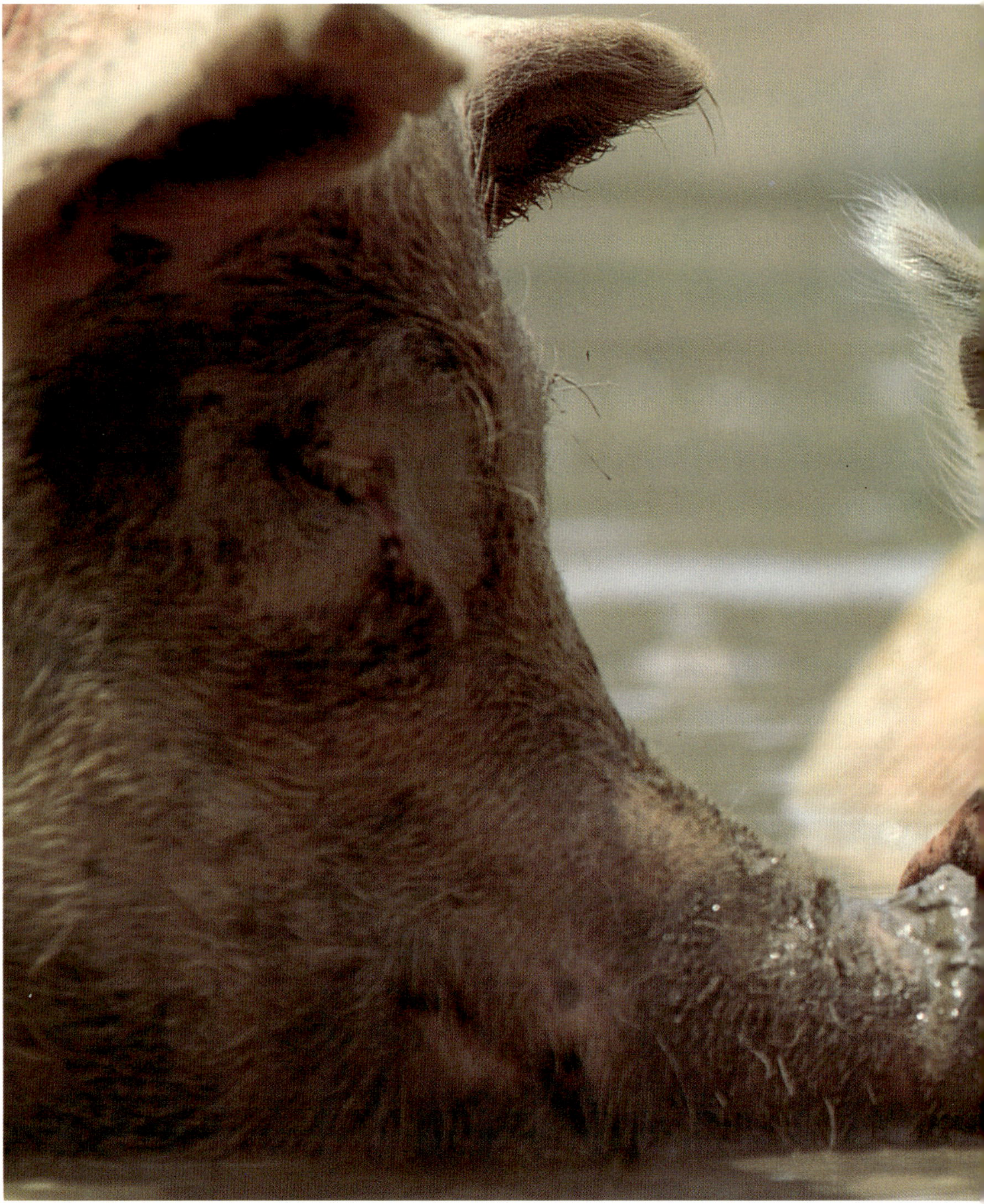

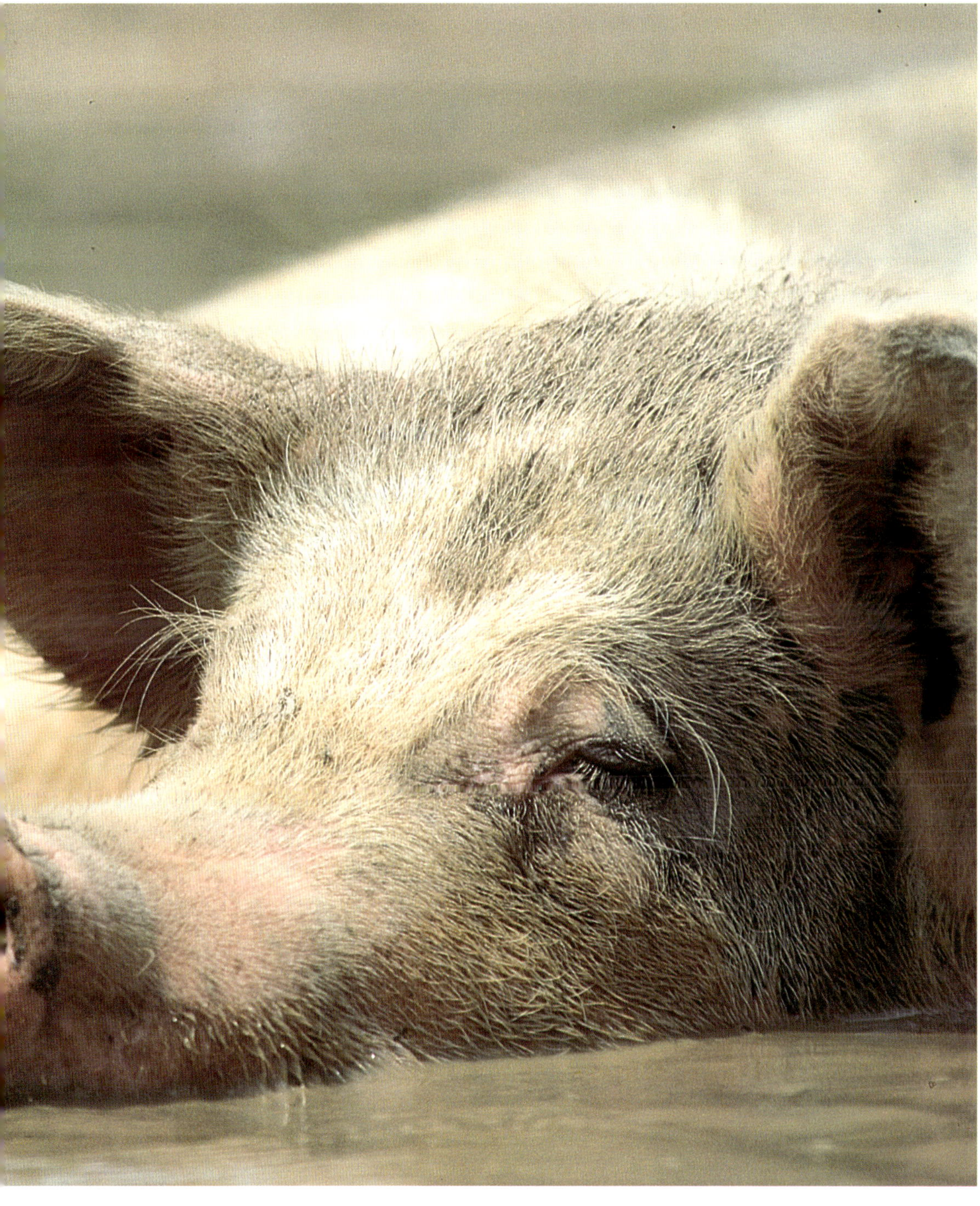

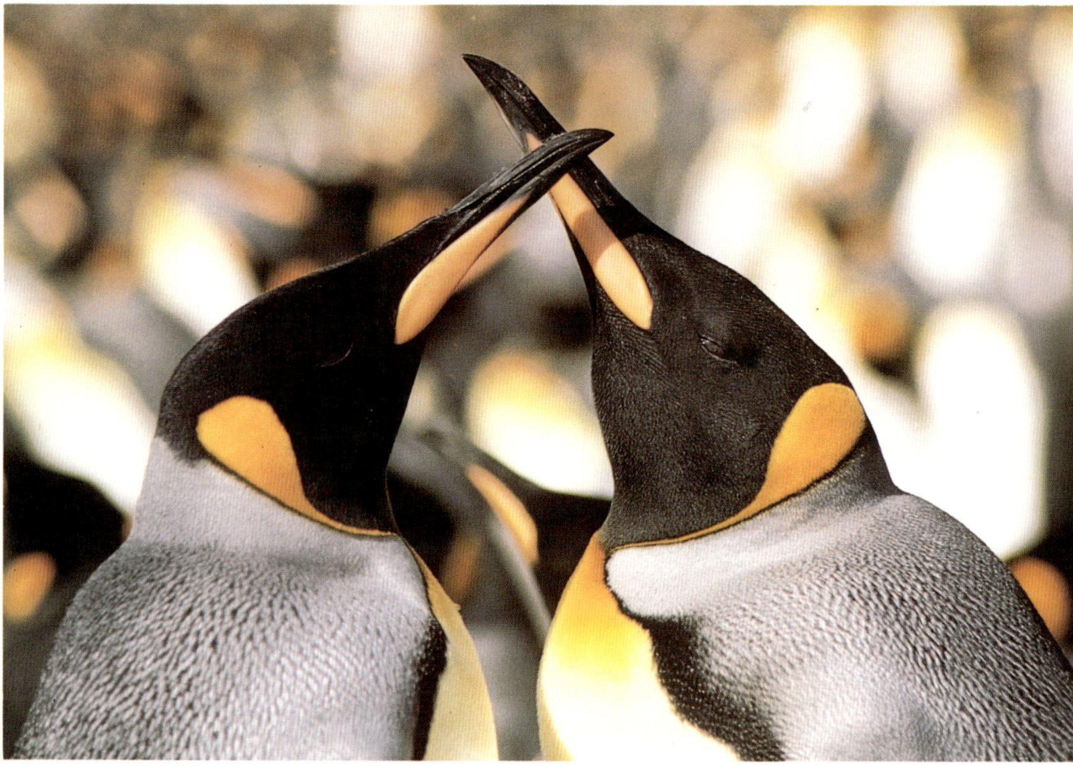

"Lord, I wonder what fool it was that first invented kissing!"

(Jonathan Swift)

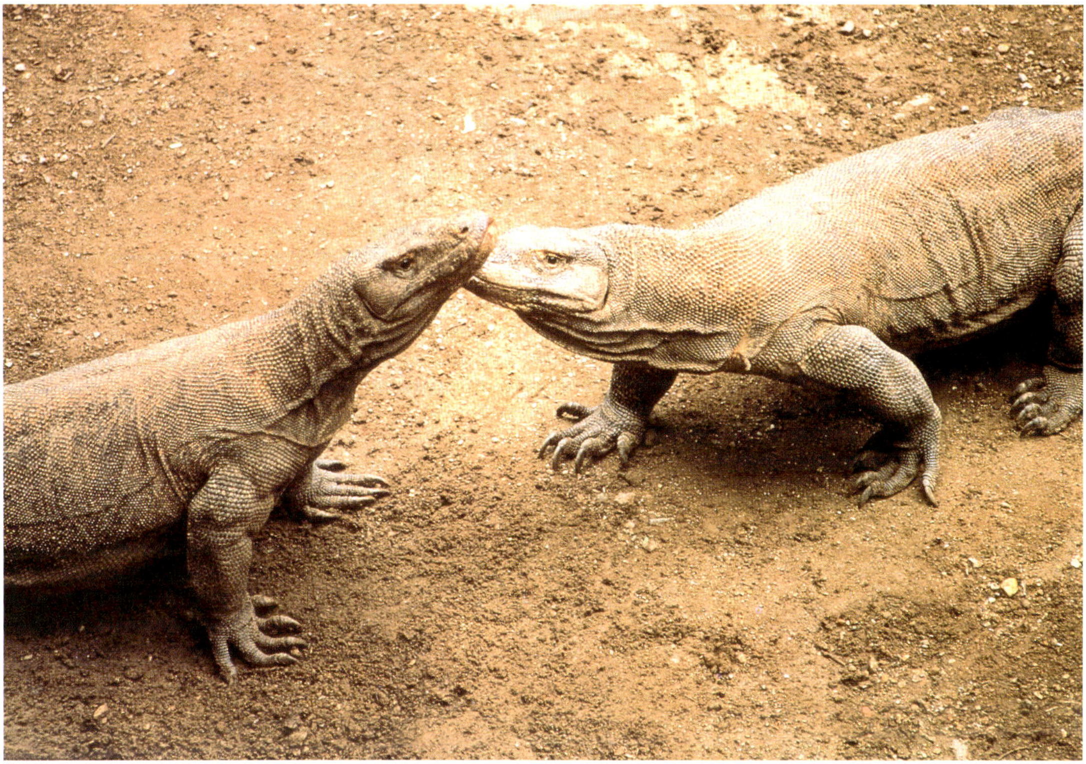

"Be plain in dress, and sober in your diet;
In short, my deary! kiss me, and be quiet."

(Lady Mary Wortley Montagu)

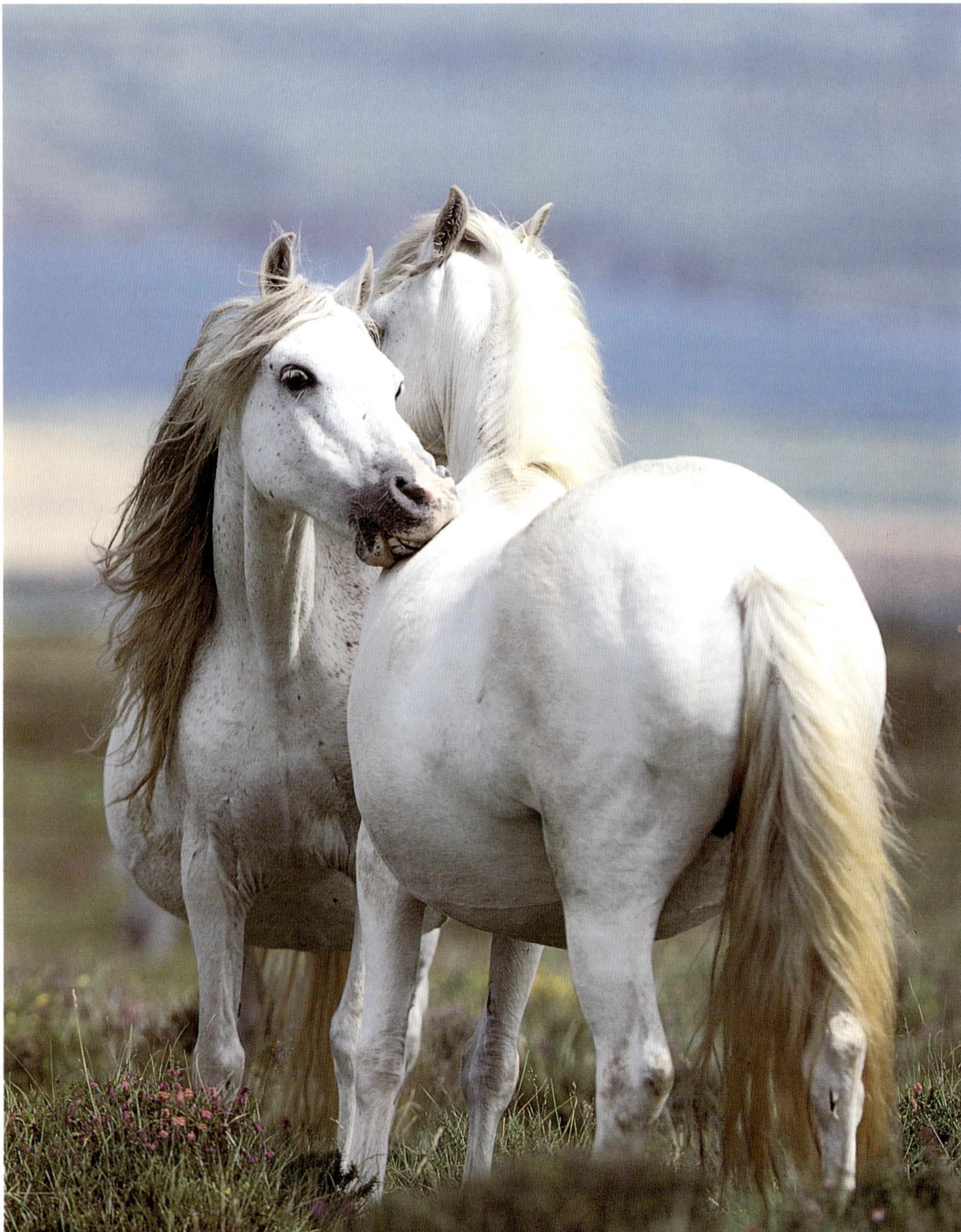

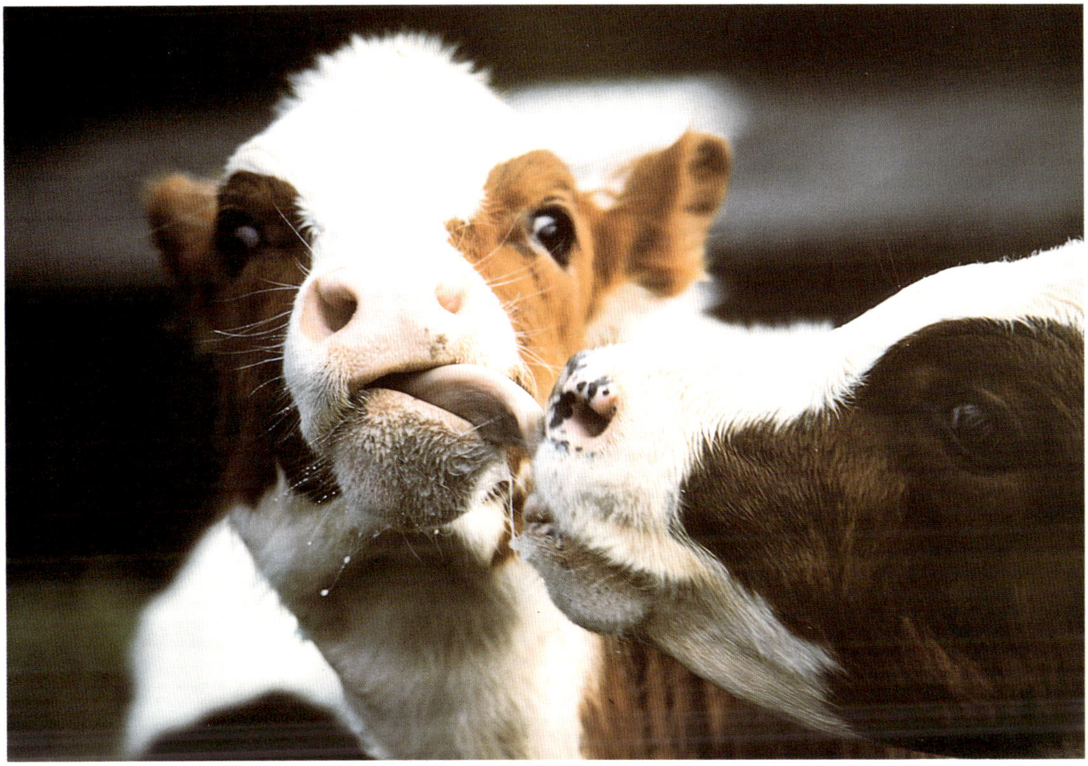

"Mouths that crave to kiss
Tongues that thirst to lick
Consume me in your desire"

(Maryam Sachs)

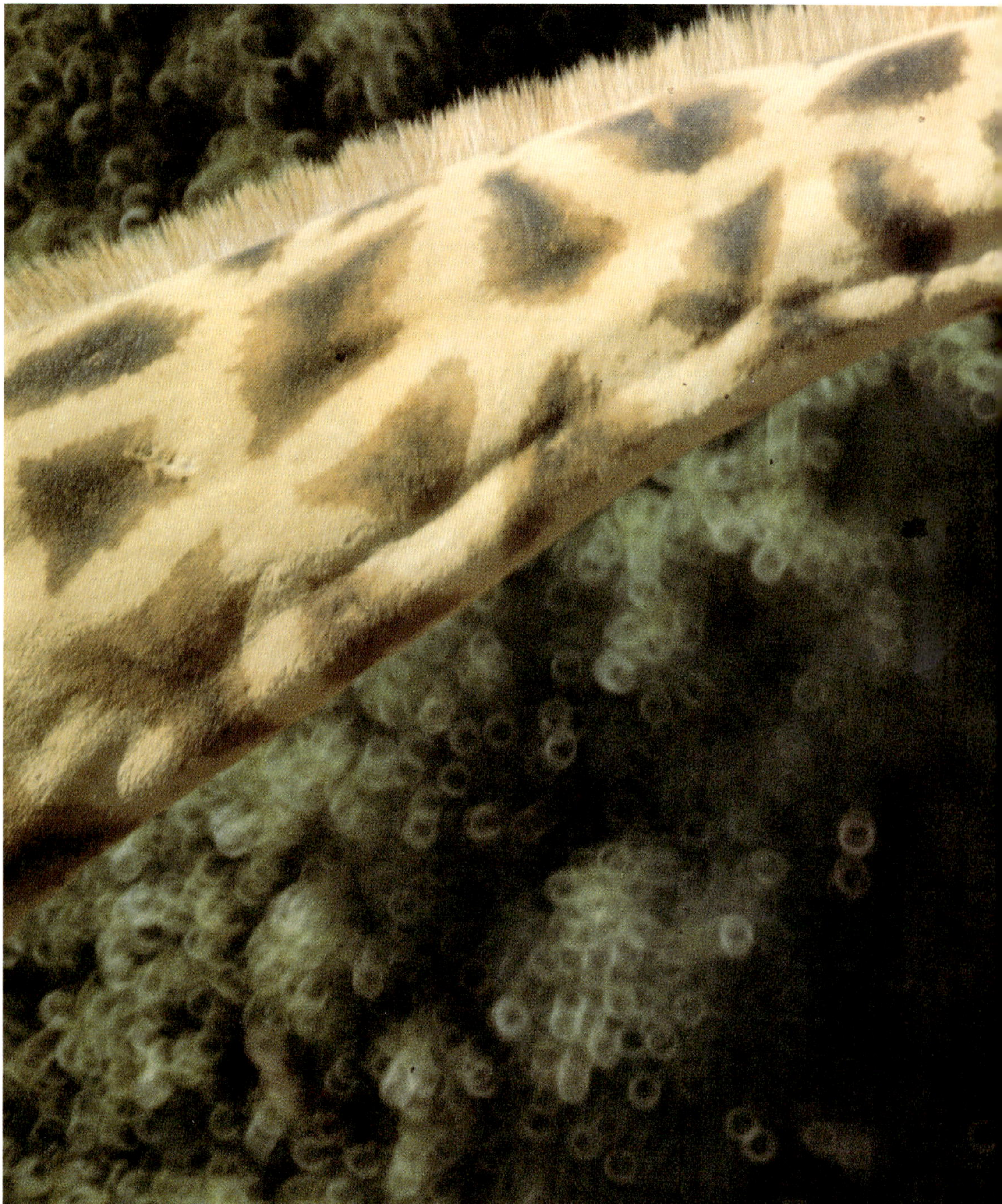

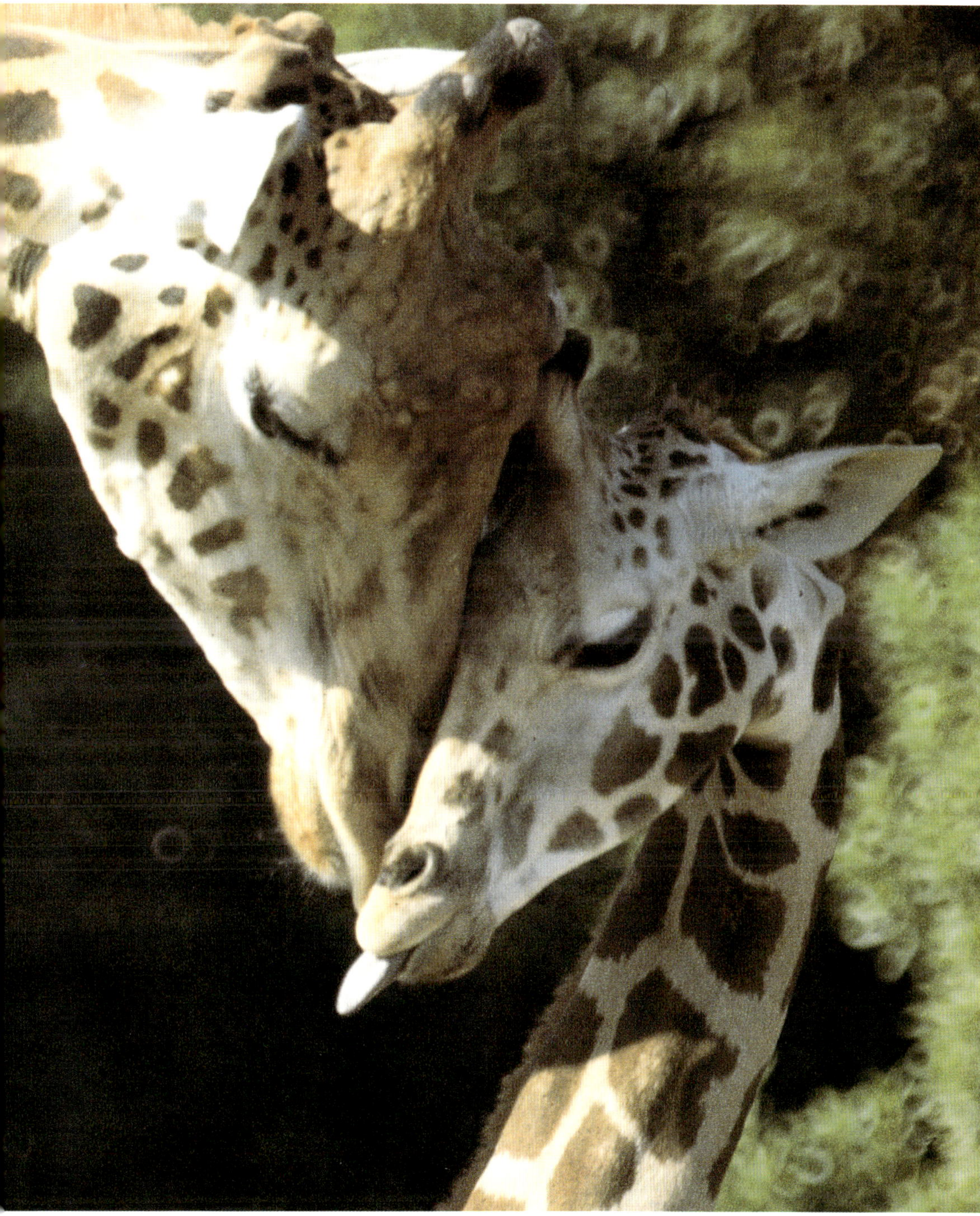

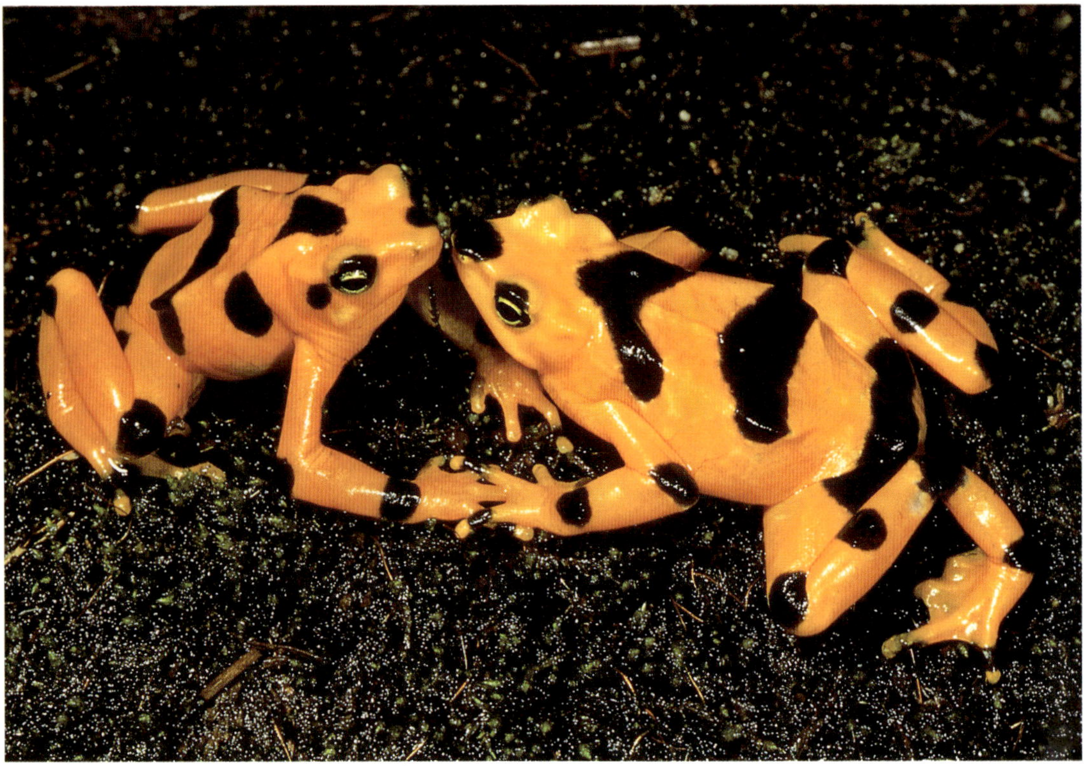

"A frog he would a-wooing go."

(English nursery rhyme)

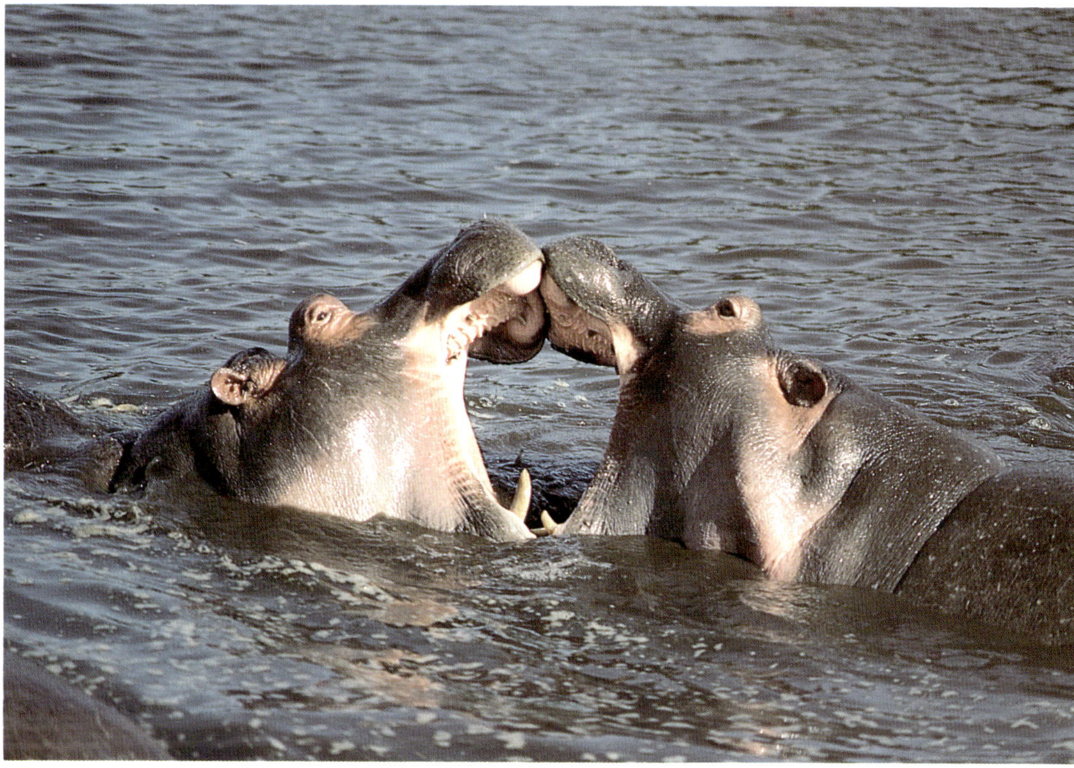

"Then come kiss me, sweet and twenty."

(William Shakespeare)

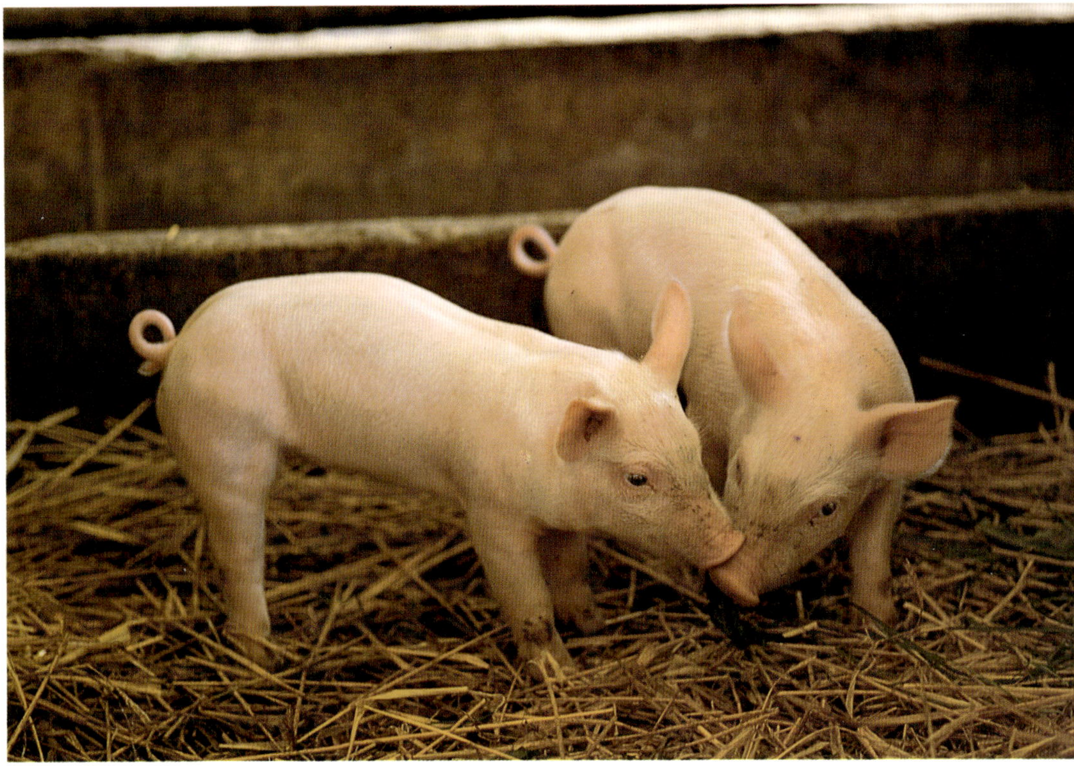

Do you want to know a secret?

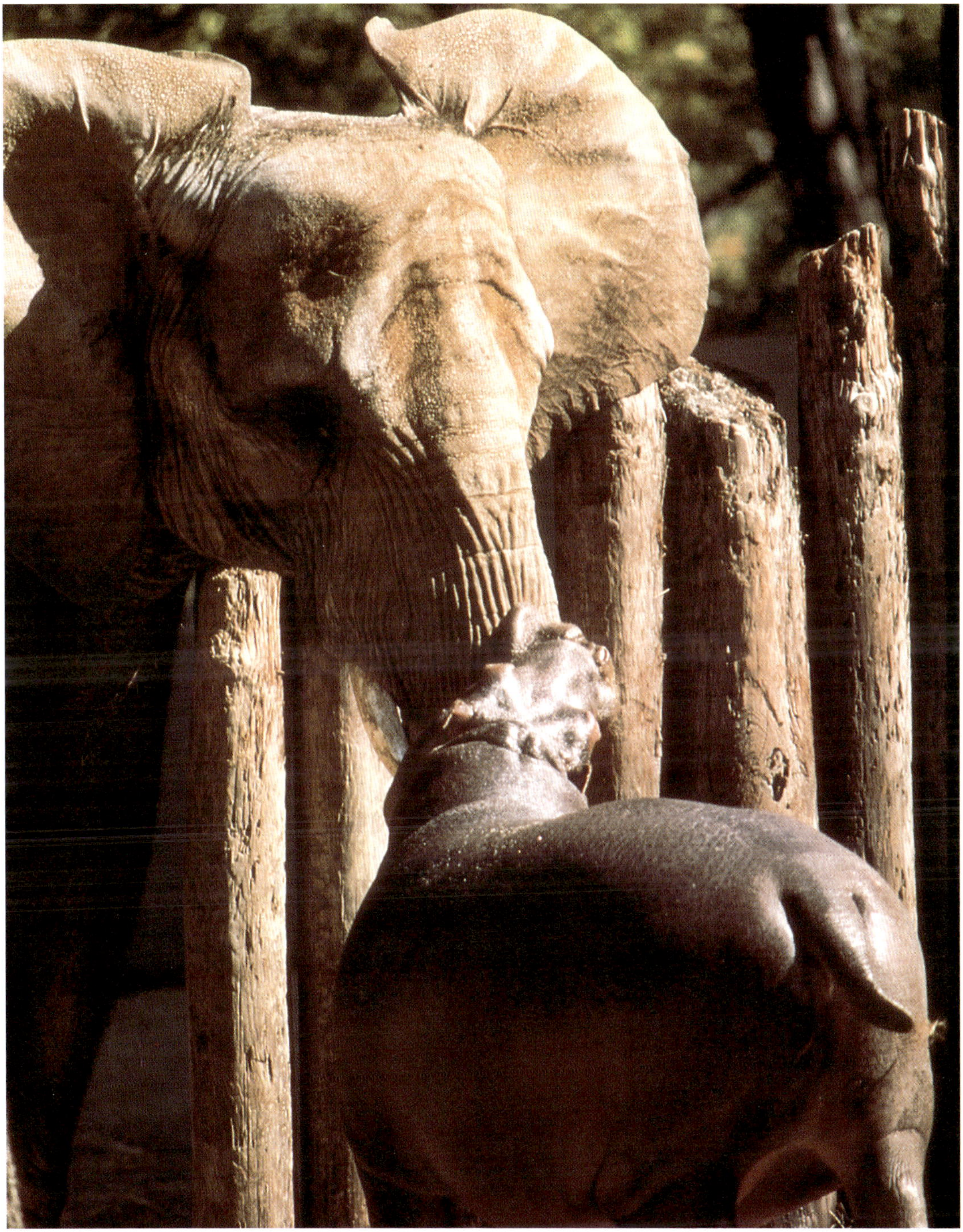

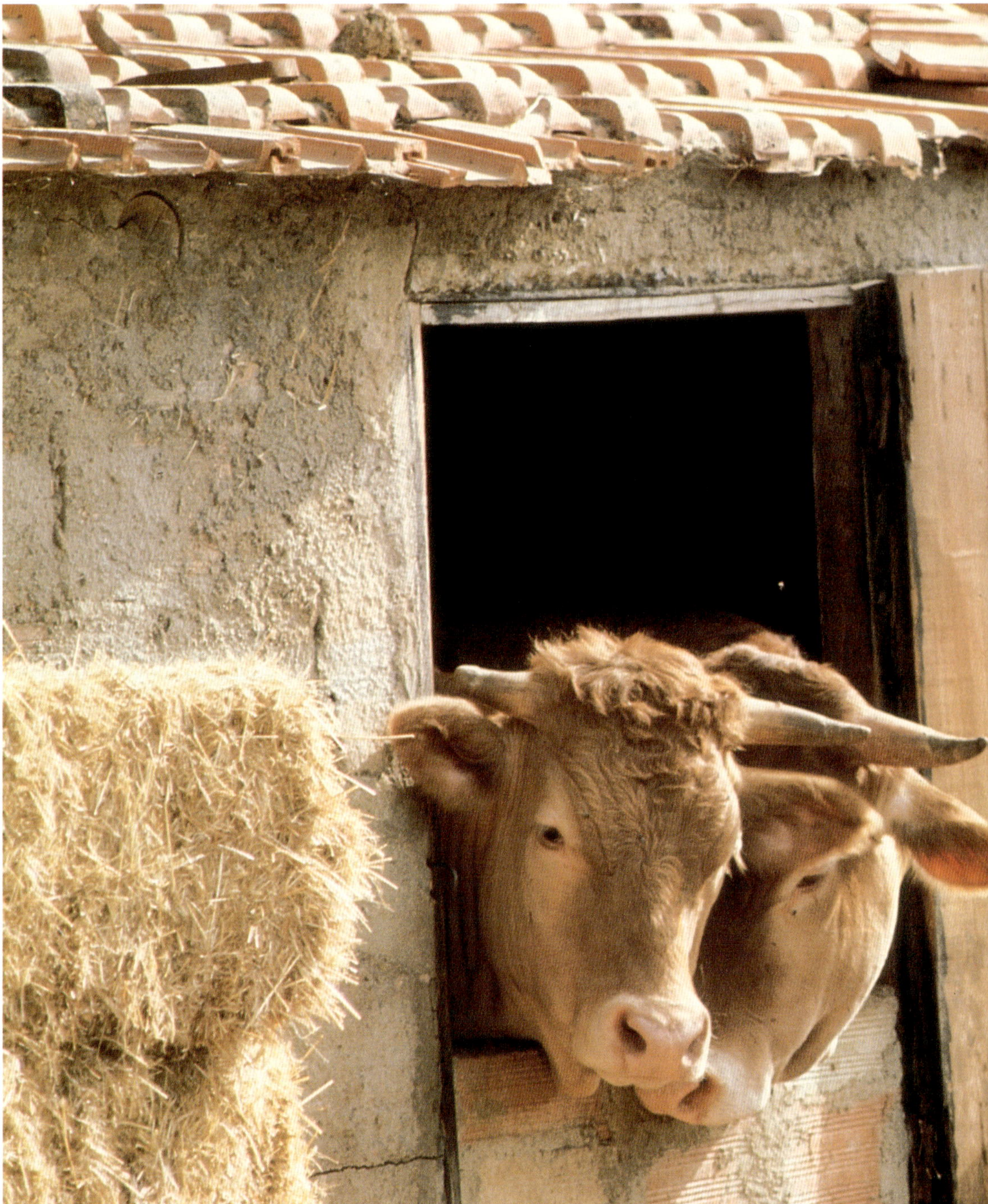

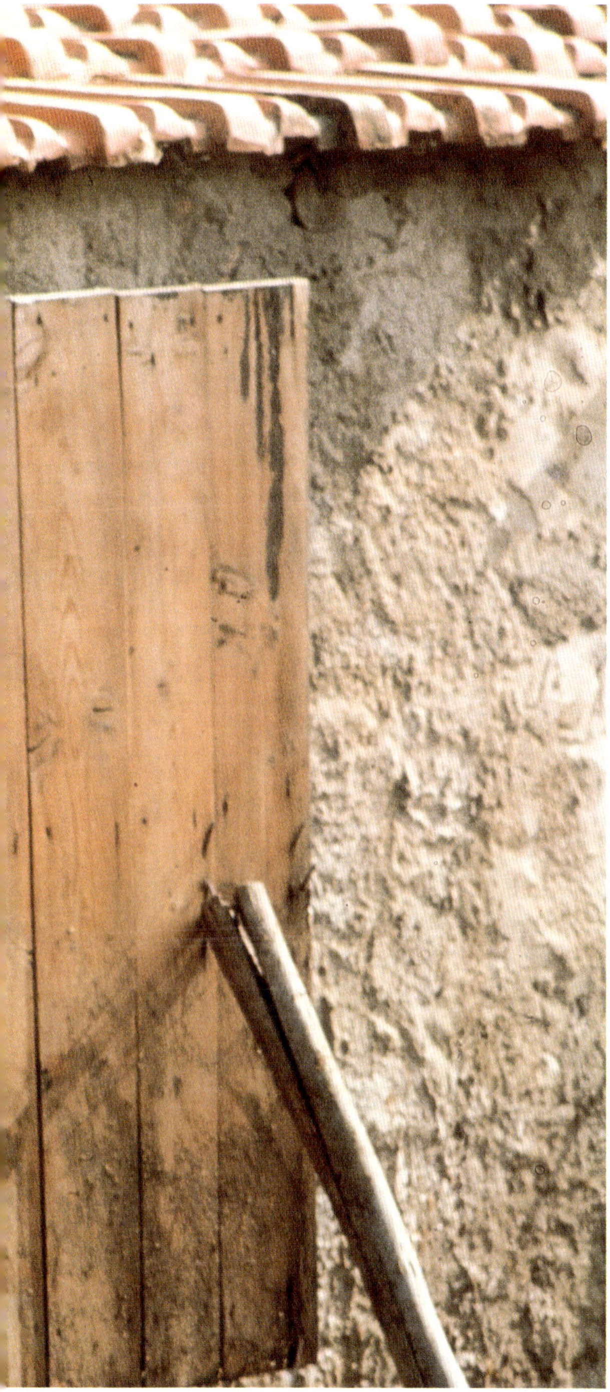

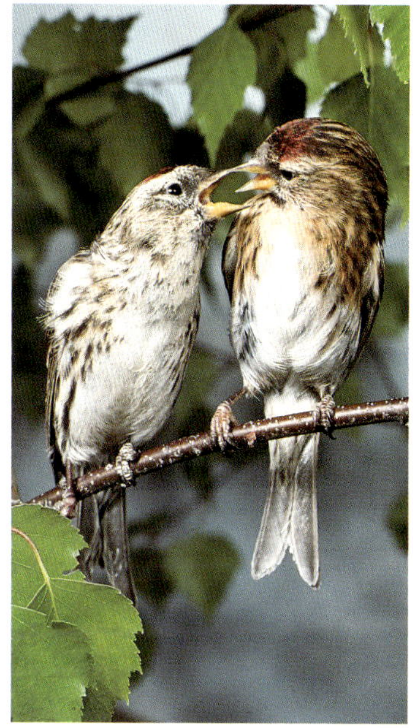

"Kissing like a beginner takes a lot of experience."

(Zsa Zsa Gabor)

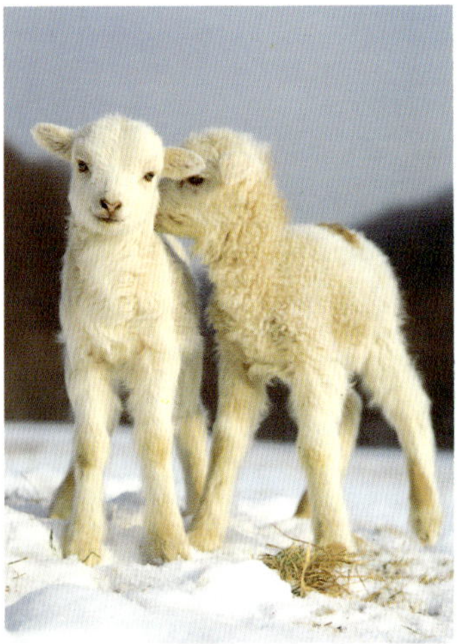

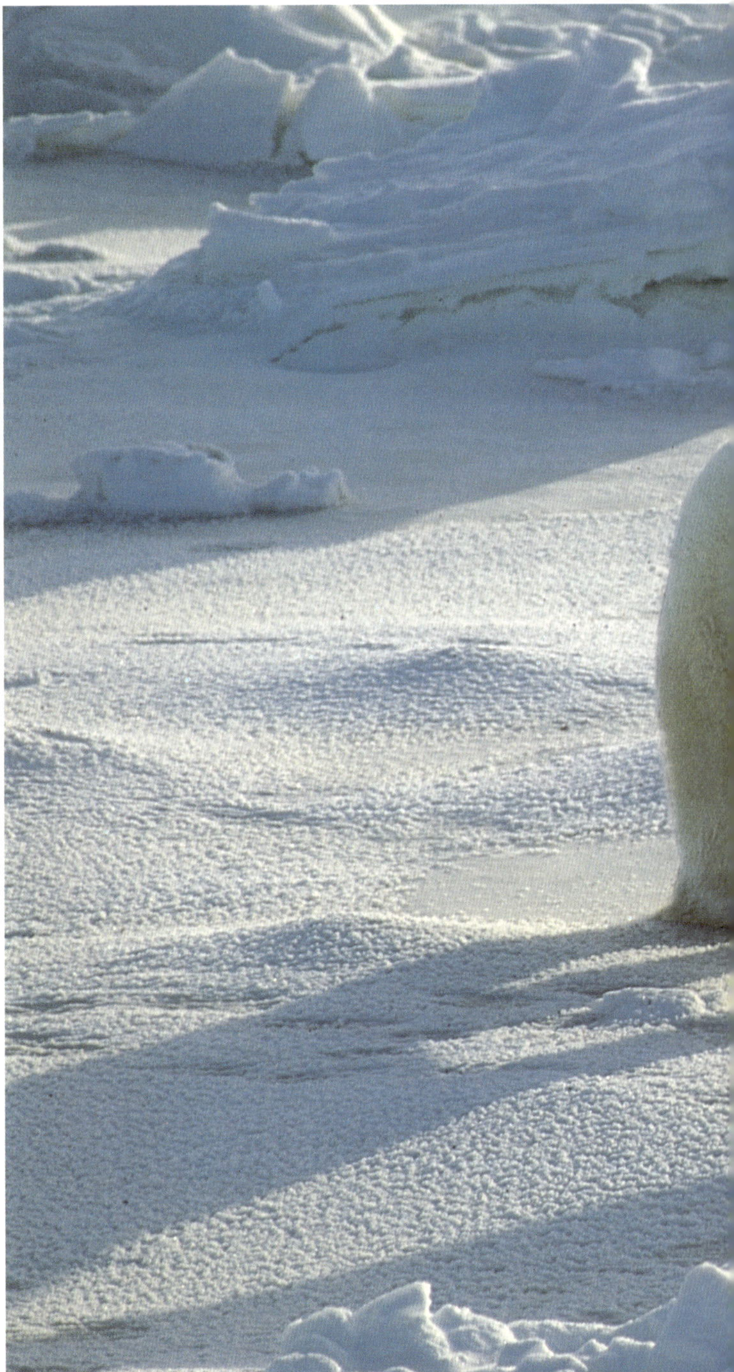

Softly softly

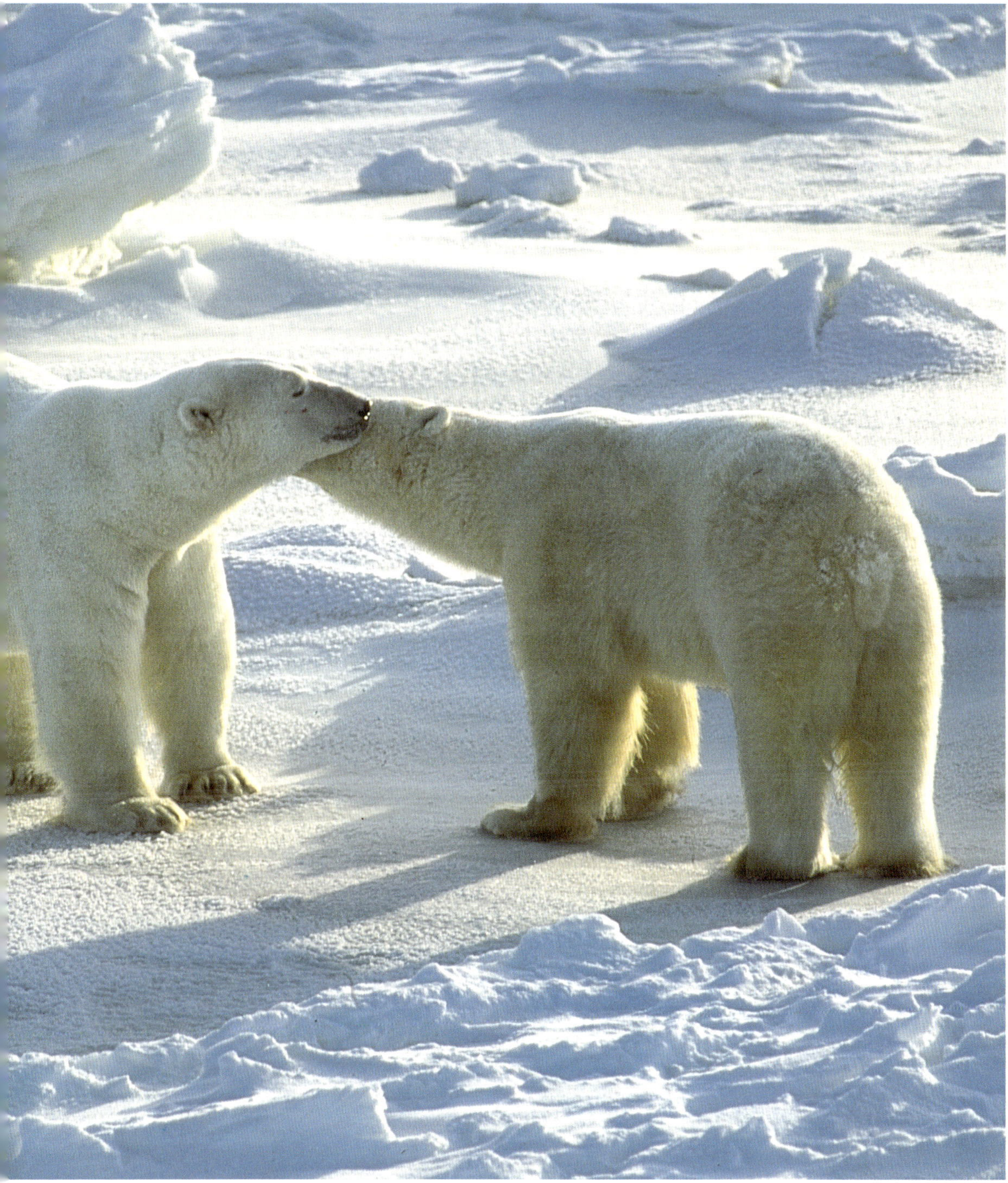

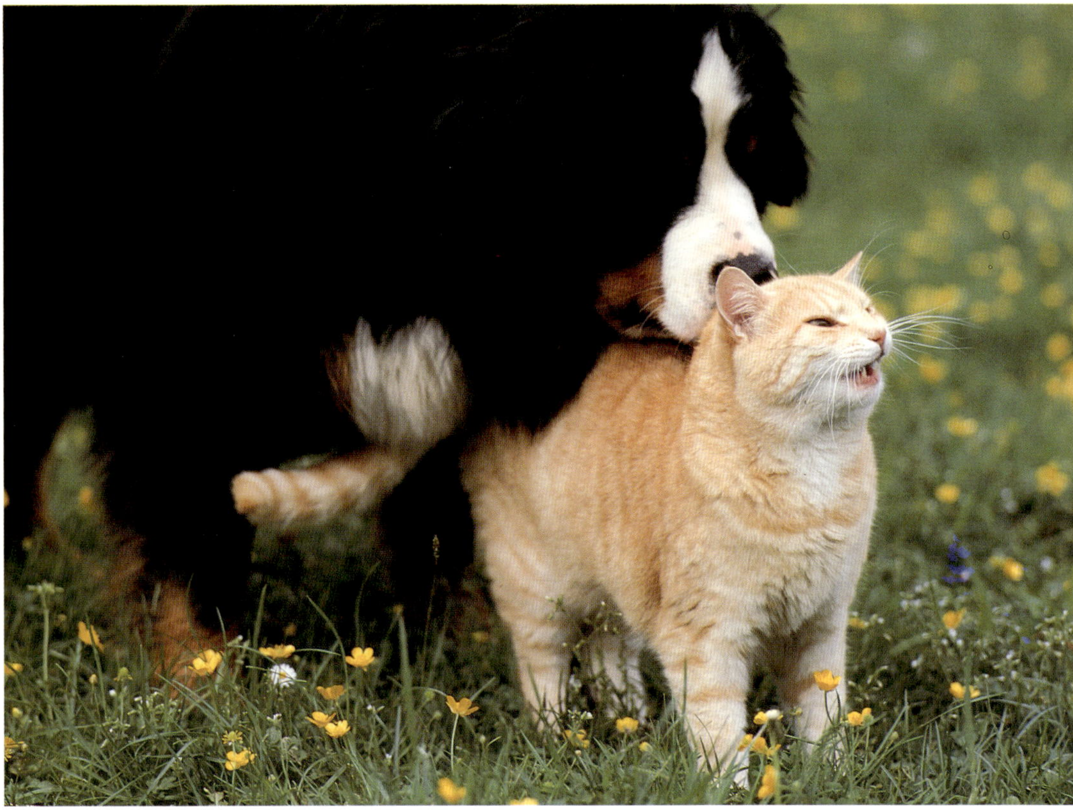

"A most loving, kissing, kind-hearted gentleman."

(William Cowper)

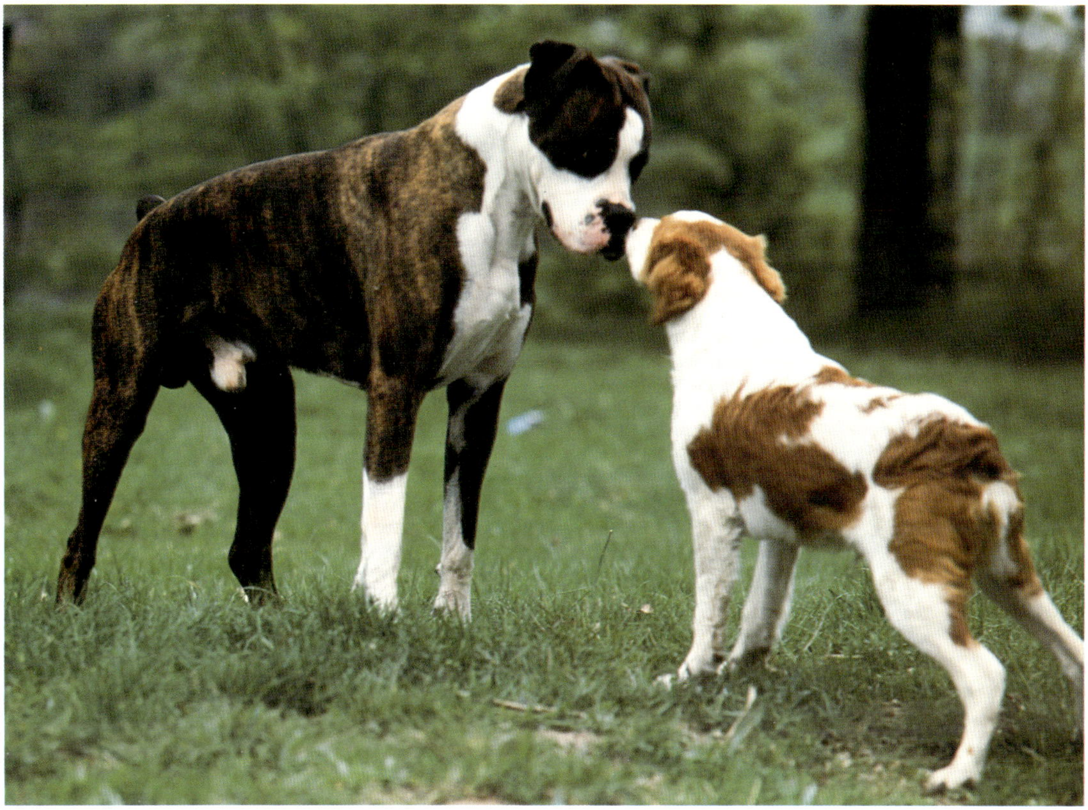

"If only I could tell
What flutters in my soul!
Our kisses and our words
Are grown into a whole."

(Heinrich Heine)

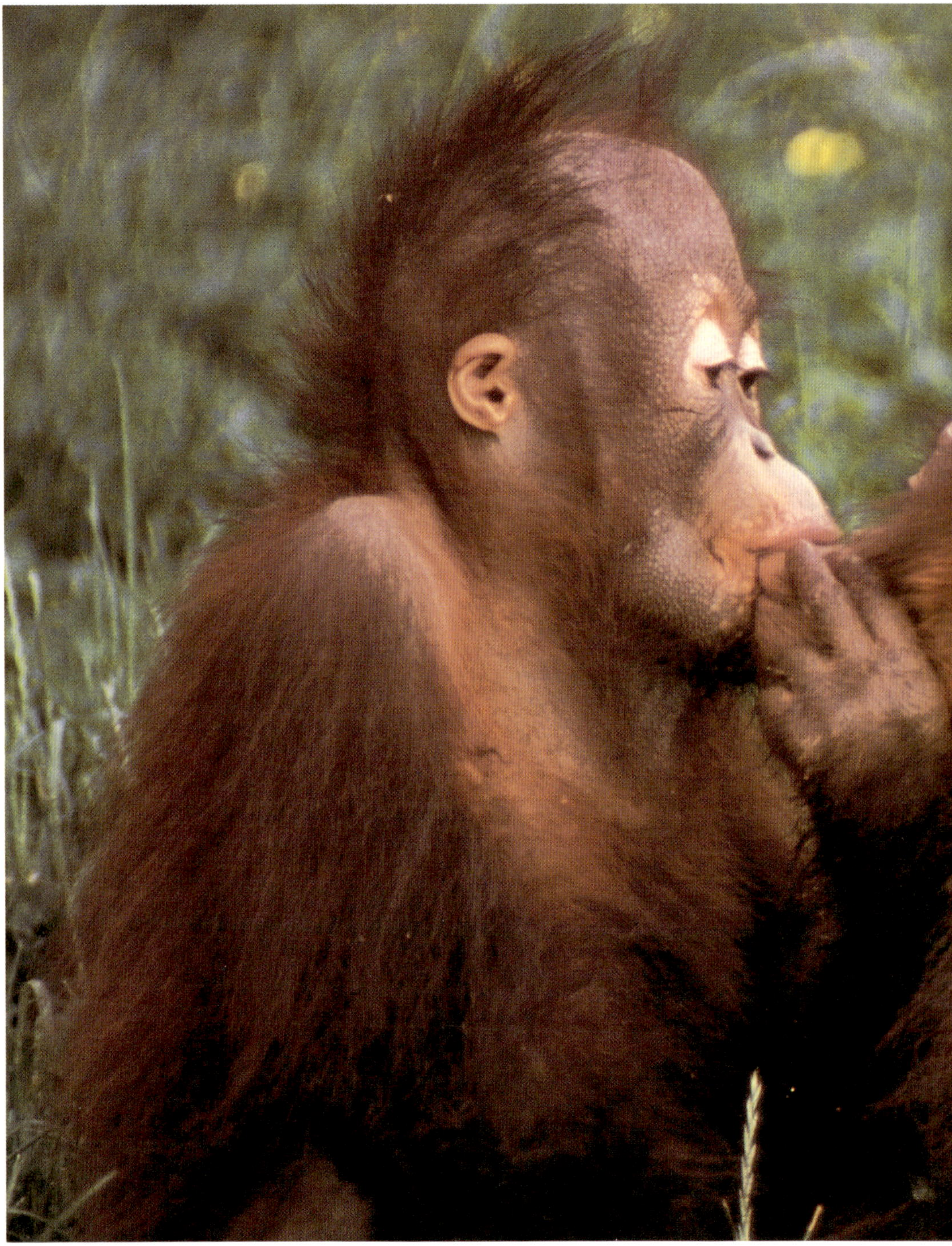

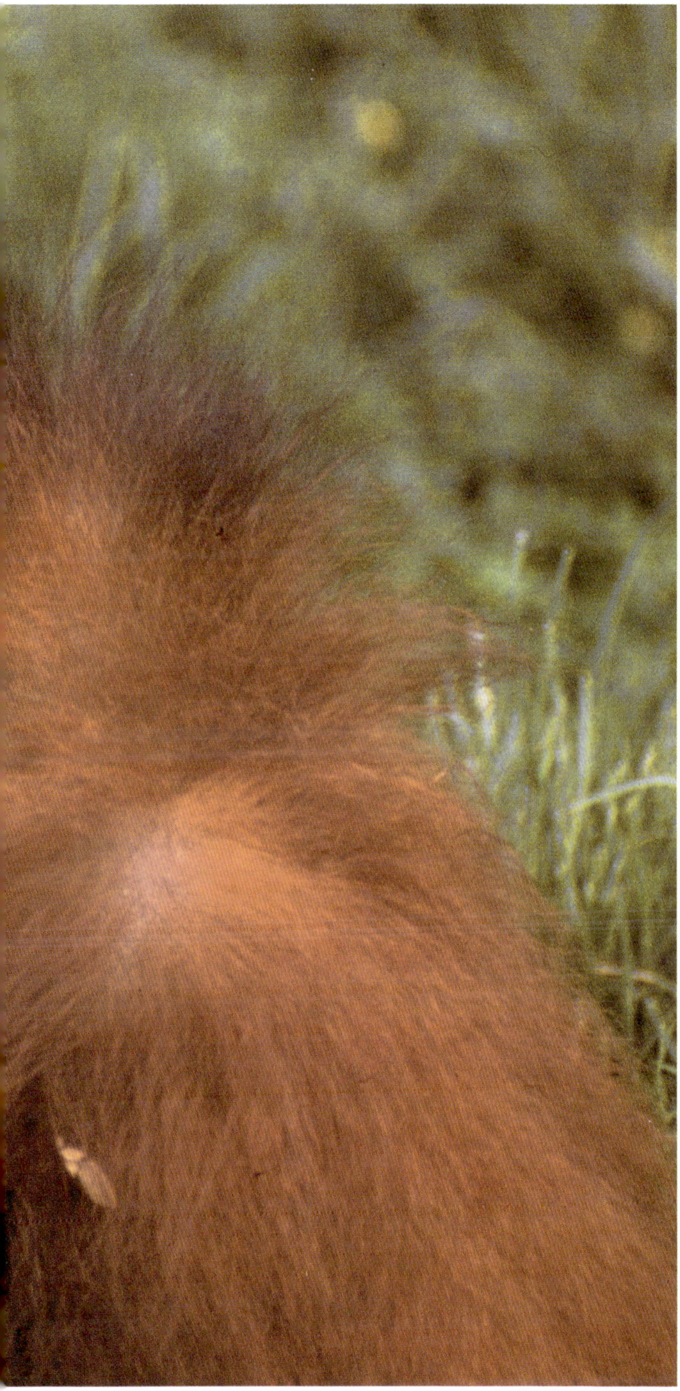

Monkey business

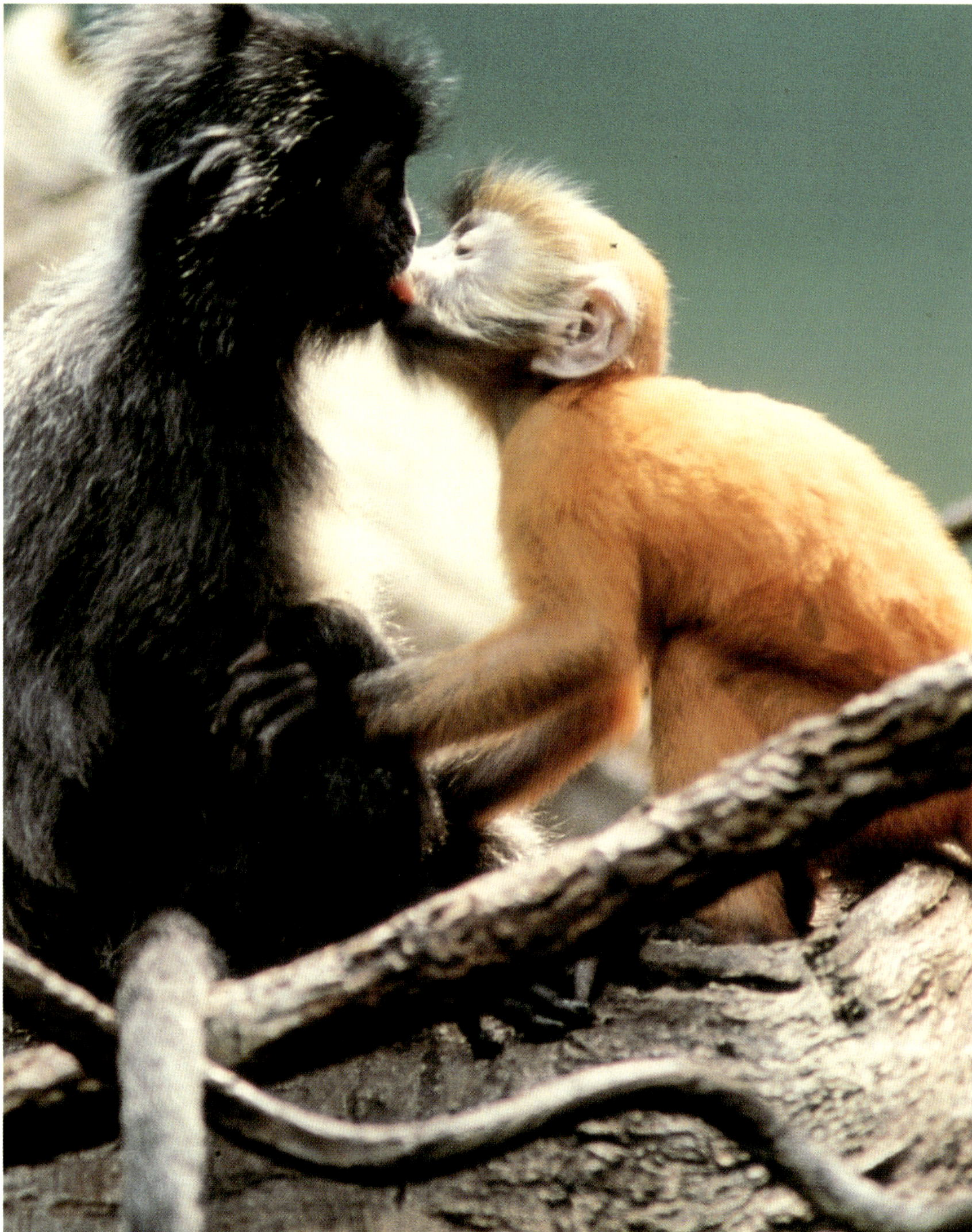

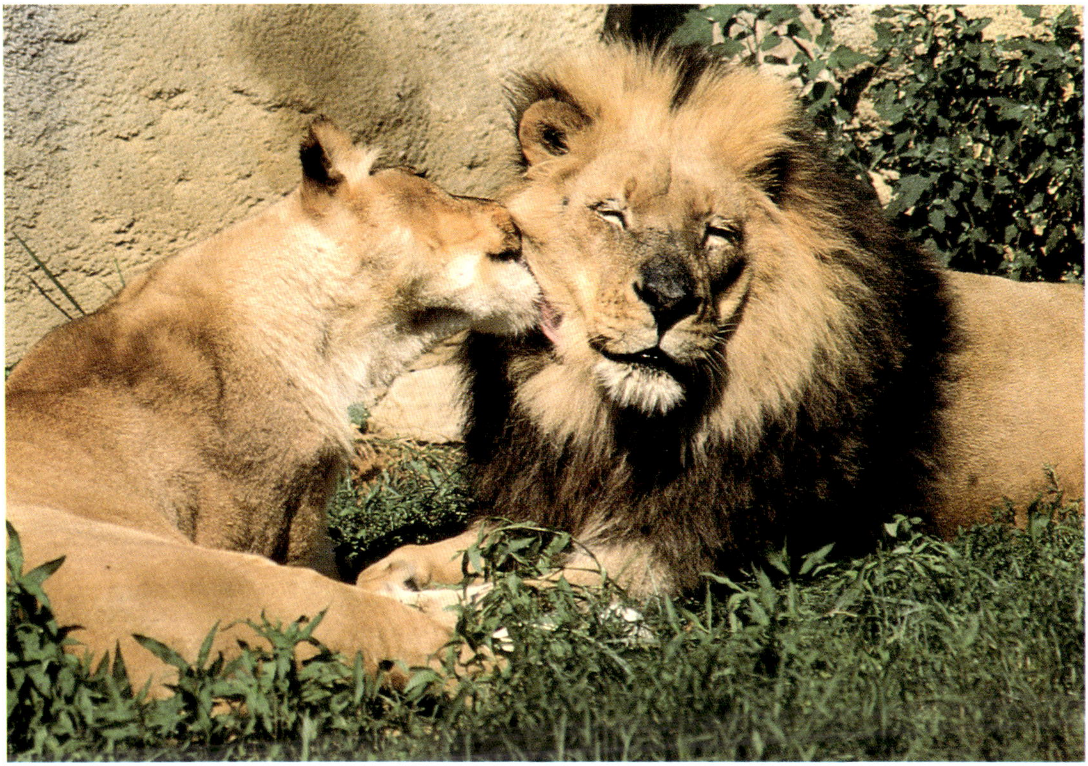

"Come live with me and be my love."

(Christopher Marlowe)

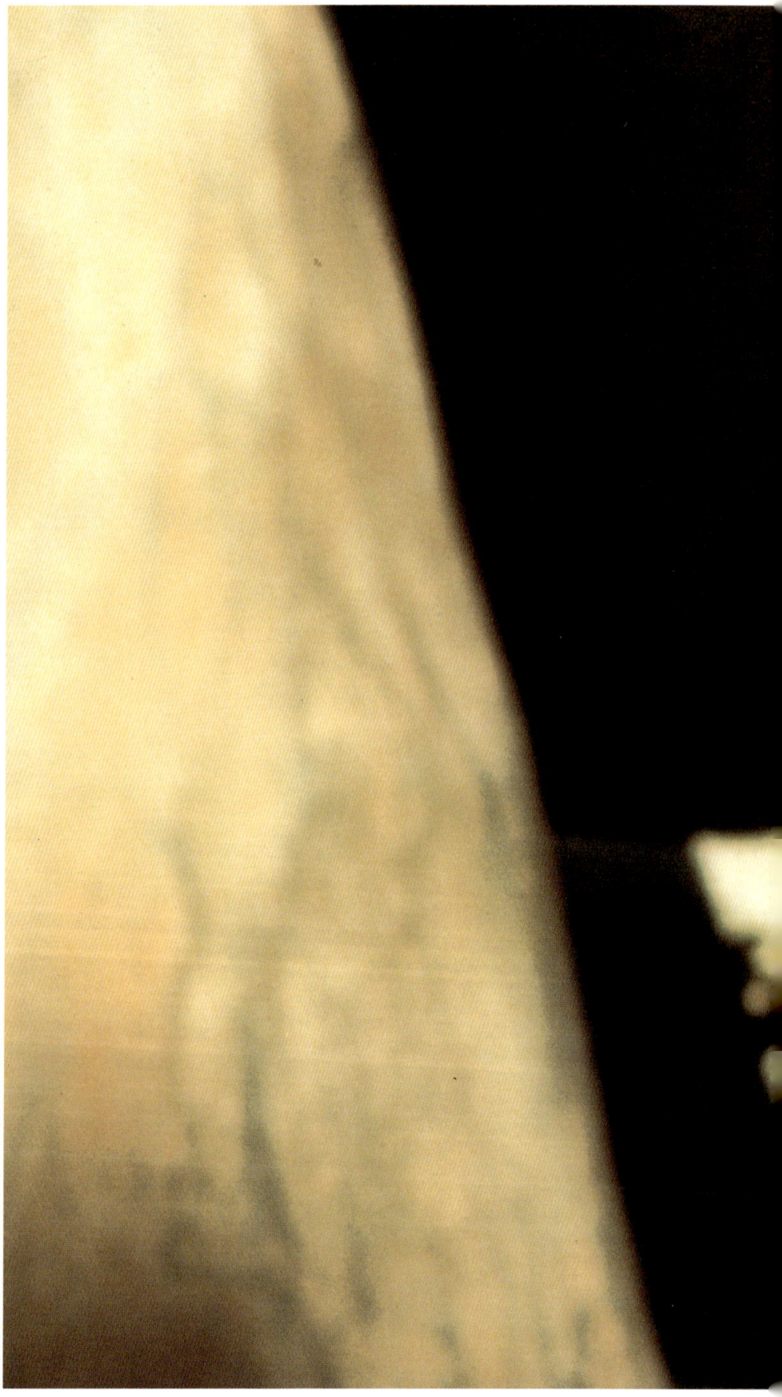

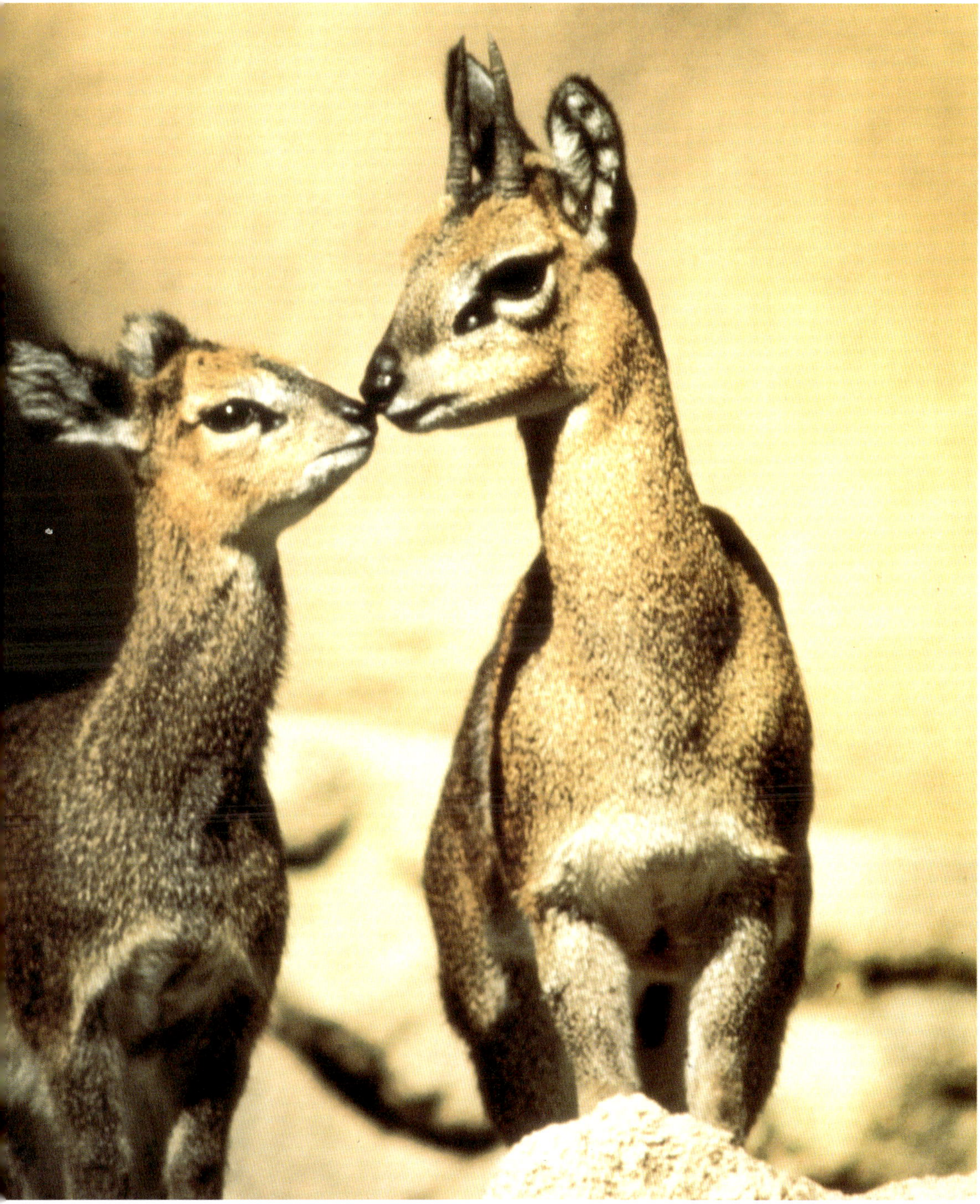

Who was that canoodling?

Photo credits

© Animals, Animals (Ray Richardson 6, J.H. Robinson 9, John Chellman 14, David C. Fritts 17, Johnny Johnson 20, Zig Leszczynski 81, Michael Dick 91, John Nees 92-93)
© Ardea London Ltd., London (Masahiro Tijima 29, Liz Bonford, Cover, 38, François Gohier 84-85)
© Bavaria Bildagentur, Düsseldorf (Stock Imagery 46, 69, TCL 72)
© David Keith Jones / Images of Africa Photo Bank (37, 79)
© Helga Lade Fotoagentur GmbH, Frankfurt/Main (Hans Rohr 48-49, Bernd Siering 50, R. Sebastian 73)
© IFA-Bilderteam, Munich (Aberham 18, P.A.N. 26-27, 34, Amadeus 28, UPA 31, BCI 32-33, 36, 39, 42, 82-83, 90, Köpfle 43, Fritz Pölking 57, 58-59, R. Maier 74, Birgit Koch 80, Chytry 88-89)
© Interfoto, Munich (Essler 47, Fritz Prenzel 51, M. Weinzierl 63)
© Mauritius, Stuttgart (Photothèque SDP 56)
© Bildarchiv Okapia, Frankfurt/Main (NAS/T. McHugh 23, Lanceau 30, Jeff Foott 55, Hans Reinhard 66, 67, 83, 84, 86)
© Suzanne Schapowalow, Hamburg (Ramaekers 40, 75, 87, mat 61)
© The Image Bank, Munich (Stuart Dee, Backcover, 5, Gary Faber 62, Jack Bauer 76-77, James H. Carmichael 78)
© Volker Ernst, Berlin (W. Sittig 12-13, 44-45, 52-53)
© ZEFA, Düsseldorf (T. Fitzharris 35, Meyers 40-41, 54, Tom McHugh 60, Art Wolfe 64-65, Gay Bumgarner 68, Perla 70-71)

In this series:

- Audubon
- Blossfeldt
- Dürer
- von Gloeden
- Kissing Animals
- Larsson
- Mollino
- Mucha
- Naughty Paris
- Plüschow
- Rodin